AI for Beginners Made Easy

Master Artificial Intelligence from
Generative AI to Machine Learning -
Turbocharge Your Career & Productivity With
Interactive Exercises in 7 Days or Less

Alex Bennett

Global Ink Publishing

Contents

Introduction

Have you ever used a GPS to navigate through unfamiliar streets? It's like that when you start to explore the world of Artificial Intelligence (AI). At first, it seems daunting, as if you're venturing into a maze of technical jargon and complex theories meant only for the initiated. But just as GPS guides you turn by turn, this book aims to lead you through the AI landscape with simplicity and clarity, ensuring you feel as comfortable with AI as you do with using your smartphone.

My own foray into the world of AI was a rollercoaster ride filled with moments of confusion and revelation. I was using various tools in my business, oblivious to the fact that they were powered by AI! From the handy, quick reply suggestions in Gmail to the game-changing Grammarly for editing and enhancing manuscripts, AI was all around me. The turning point in my understanding came when I realized that AI isn't just a tool for tech wizards but a transformative technology that touches all our lives, much like the internet did. Do you remember the thrill of setting up your first email? That's the same exhilaration I experienced when I ran my first AI program. It's this sense of accomplishment that I want to share with you.

However, many people are hesitant to embrace AI due to prevalent misconceptions. Some believe "AI is only for tech wizards" or "It's too late to start learning about AI." Let me assure you, these notions are far from reality. AI is a tool for everyone, and the present is the perfect time to start exploring it. This book will demonstrate just how practical and relevant AI can be, even for those who have never written a line of code and have no plans to do so.

The purpose of this book is crystal clear. It's written to demystify AI, making it understandable and applicable in everyday life while equipping you with the knowledge to navigate the evolving job market. We'll delve into generative AI, a powerful tool that can create content from simple prompts, and explore how it differs from ChatGPT, which is primarily designed for conversation. Understanding these distinctions is vital as they open up a world of diverse possibilities and applications.

The reality is that AI is reshaping the job landscape. Studies predict that while some jobs may be automated, many more will be created. This book aims to prepare you for these shifts and inspire you to embrace them proactively.

To guide you through this exciting journey, this book is structured into eight main chapters, each focusing on a key aspect of AI:

1. Understanding AI Fundamentals: This chapter lays the groundwork by explaining basic AI concepts, its evolution, and how it mimics human intelligence.

2. Overcoming Challenges in AI Learning: We address common challenges faced by beginners, offer strategies to overcome them, and discuss the importance of AI ethics.

3. Generative AI and Its Creative Potential: Here, we explore the fascinating world of generative AI, its applications in creative fields, and the ethical considerations surrounding it.

4. AI in Everyday Life: This chapter showcases how AI is already integrated into our daily lives, from personalized online experiences to smart homes and healthcare.

5. AI Tools and Resources for Beginners: This chapter is your go-to guide for the best AI tools and resources available, helping you navigate the wealth of information out there.

6. Hands-On Projects with AI: Get ready to put your knowledge into practice with a series of hands-on AI projects designed for beginners.

7. The Future of Work with AI: We explore how AI is transforming the job market, the skills needed to thrive in an AI-driven world, and the ethical considerations surrounding job displacement.

8. Advanced AI Trends and Innovations: The final chapter offers a glimpse into the exciting future of AI, covering topics like quantum computing, AI in space exploration, and the evolution of AI itself.

As we dive into these pages, expect an approachable narrative peppered with practical examples and exercises that require no experience with technology. You'll find that

AI isn't about complex algorithms and data alone; it's also about the ethical considerations that come with it. We'll discuss how to use AI responsibly and ethically, ensuring that as we harness its power, we're also mindful of its impact.

So, let's start this journey together. With straightforward explanations and hands-on guidance, I invite you to peel back the layers of Artificial Intelligence with me. This path promises insight and practical skills relevant to our changing world.

Let me share a quick story to give you an example of AI's impact. Recently, I used an AI tool to analyze data for this exact book that would have taken weeks to complete manually. The tool provided insights crucial to my target audience research in just a few minutes. What would have usually taken me days now took mere minutes, saving time and allowing me to focus on what really matters: writing this book. It's these kinds of practical applications that I look forward to exploring with you.

Welcome to your AI adventure. Let's demystify and navigate this terrain together, making AI accessible and beneficial to your everyday life.

Suggested Daily Schedule

If you have bought this book because of the "7 days" promise to master Artificial Intelligence and turbocharge your career and productivity, you can follow the recommended daily schedule below. However, if you have bought this book simply to understand AI at your own pace, feel free to ignore this completely.

Day 1 - Chapter 1, Chapter 2 & Chapter 3

Day 2 - Chapter 4 & Chapter 5

Day 3 - Create your first chatbot (Chapter 6.1)

Day 4 - Scratch for Non-Coders (Chapter 6.2)

Day 5 - AI-powered Personal Assistant with Zapier & AI For Your Personal Finance Management (Chapters 6.3 & 6.4)

Day 6 - AI-powered Blog Content Idea Generator & Basic Image Classifier (Chapters 6.5 & 6.6) - *Suggested to pick one that is most useful or interesting to you*

Day 7 - Chapter 7 & Chapter 8 + Conclusion

Chapter 1

Understanding AI Fundamentals

A rtificial Intelligence often seems like a complex, impenetrable field reserved for experts. This chapter aims to demystify AI, breaking it down into understandable components. We'll explore the fundamental concepts, uncover how AI simulates human intelligence, and delve into the fascinating world of machine learning. By the end of this chapter, you'll have a solid grasp of AI's basic principles and terminology.

1.1 Decoding AI: From Definitions to Real-World Applications

AI, or Artificial Intelligence, might sound like a fancy term reserved for scientists and sci-fi movies. Still, it's more familiar to you than you think. Essentially, AI involves machines performing tasks that typically require human intelligence. These tasks range from recognizing speech, like your smartphone does, to making decisions, similar to how your car's GPS chooses the best route home, and many far more complex assignments.

Now, there's a spectrum here—from 'narrow AI,' designed to perform specific tasks (think of your voice-activated assistant setting a timer), to 'general AI,' which is more about comprehensively mimicking human intelligence. However, we're not quite there yet. The former is all around us, enhancing our daily lives, while the latter largely remains (for now) within research labs and theoretical discussions.

It's important to note that AI fundamentally differs from traditional computer programming. In conventional programming, developers write explicit instructions for the computer to follow. With AI, the focus is on training the machine to learn and make decisions on its own based on the data it is given. This learning aspect is what sets AI apart. It enables it to tackle complex problems that would be difficult or impossible to solve with traditional programming methods.

You interact with AI more often than you realize. It's in the recommendations Netflix makes for you, based on shows you've watched before, or how Facebook recognizes your friends' faces in a photo. AI powers the smart replies in your Gmail, helping you respond to emails faster. It is also the brain behind voice assistants like Siri or Alexa, making it easier to get information or control your smart home devices with just your voice.

In the realm of transportation, AI is revolutionizing how we move. Self-driving cars use AI to make real-time decisions that ensure the safety of the passengers by navigating roads and avoiding potential hazards. Airlines use AI to optimize flight routes, reduce fuel consumption, and predict maintenance needs for aircrafts. These applications make our lives more convenient and contribute to increased efficiency and sustainability.

This kind of AI is woven into the fabric of our everyday technologies, making them more efficient and more responsive to our needs. For example, think about spam filters in your email. They learn from the kinds of emails you mark as junk. Over time, they get better at automatically moving annoying emails out of your inbox without you having to lift a finger. That's AI at work—no drama, just quietly making your day a little less cluttered.

So, how does this all come together? Well, AI systems are fed data—lots of it. They analyze this data to identify patterns and make decisions. Take the spam filter example; by understanding the common features of emails you mark as spam, the system learns to filter similar future emails automatically.

This process is less about creating robots that think like humans and more about solving specific problems efficiently. By demystifying how AI applications work, we can start to see AI as a helpful tool rather than an ominous, overwhelming force that will take over the world.

There's no shortage of myths about AI. Many believe that AI is only for tech geniuses or that it's inherently biased and dangerous. While AI does pose new challenges and ethical questions, understanding its limitations and capabilities helps us use it better.

For instance, AI is only as good as the data it receives. If the data is biased, the AI's decisions will be too. However, by being aware of these limitations, developers can work to improve AI systems, making them not only smarter but also fairer.

Knowing this helps clarify AI and highlights the importance of human oversight in these systems.

Understanding the basics of AI doesn't require an engineering degree—just curiosity and a willingness to learn. As we continue to illustrate AI, you'll see how it's not just a tool for the few but a part of everyday life that all of us can use and benefit from. And who knows? Maybe the next AI tool could be something you help create, bringing your unique perspective to the table.

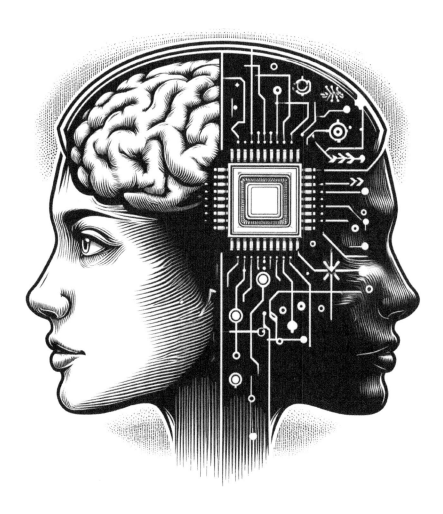

1.2 The Evolution of AI: A Journey Through Time

When we talk about the evolution of AI, it's a story of gradual, persistent growth sprinkled with some serious growth spurts. The roots of AI can be traced way back to the mid-20th century when computers filled entire rooms and had less processing power than your modern-day calculator. One of the first significant milestones came in the 1950s when Alan Turing, a British polymath, introduced the Turing Test—a method for determining whether or not a machine is capable of thinking like a human. This experiment was less about building intelligent machines at the time and more about understanding human cognition.

Fast-forward to 1997, a watershed moment when IBM's Deep Blue defeated world chess champion Garry Kasparov. It wasn't just a win in a game; it symbolized machines' capabilities to perform tasks that require intelligence, strategy, and foresight. Then came the 21st century, and with it, Google's algorithm improvements, revolutionizing how we retrieve information. It's been a domino effect ever since, with each breakthrough inspiring another, leading us to sophisticated AI like Siri, Alexa, and beyond.

The technological advancements that have propelled AI are nothing short of extraordinary. Consider the exponential increase in computational power, elegantly described by Moore's Law, which "observed that the number of transistors on a microchip doubles about every two years, though the cost of computers is halved." Then, there's the advent of big data. In an era where every click, swipe, and "like" generates data, AI systems have become adept at pattern recognition and decision-making at speeds and accuracies that dwarf human capabilities. These technologies have not only advanced AI but have also made it increasingly omnipresent in our daily lives, integrating into systems and services we use every day.

AI's reach is vast and varied when looking at the societal impacts. In healthcare, AI algorithms help diagnose diseases such as cancer more accurately and at earlier stages than ever, potentially saving countless lives through early intervention. In finance, algorithms manage investments and detect fraudulent transactions with a precision that significantly reduces risk and enhances efficiency. And let's not forget entertainment, where AI curates personal playlists and movie recommendations, catering to individual tastes—a feature many of us have grown to love and expect.

Speculating on the future of AI can stir up a cocktail of excitement and apprehension. The possibilities seem endless. AI might drive our cars, manage our cities, and even run our homes more smoothly. However, with great power comes great responsibility. The potential societal implications are profound. As AI takes on more tasks, what will this mean for job security? How do we ensure it makes fair decisions? The answers to these questions will shape not just the future of AI but humanity itself. As we stand on the brink of what could be the next great leap in AI, it's clear that our relationship with technology will define the coming decades. The evolution of AI, much like any significant change, promises to be a mixed bag of remarkable benefits and challenges that we must be prepared to face.

1.3 How AI Mimics Human Intelligence: Unveiling the Magic

Imagine you're learning to make a perfect cup of coffee. At first, you might fumble with the proportions—too much water, not enough coffee grounds, maybe you overheat the milk. But as you keep trying, you learn from each mistake. You adjust, taste, and refine your technique until you sip your creation one day and think, "Wow, that's just right!"

AI systems work under a similar concept, particularly those designed to emulate human cognitive functions. They process vast amounts of data, learn from patterns, and make decisions based on that learning. For instance, consider AI used in predictive texting on your phone. It observes the words you type frequently, the context in which you use them, and how sentences are structured. Over time, it predicts what word you might type next. It's not just about guessing; it's about understanding language patterns and user habits—much like how you've learned to anticipate a friend's responses in a conversation.

But here's where it gets even more intriguing. AI doesn't just learn; it also reasons and solves problems. Take autonomous vehicles, for example. These cars use AI to interpret sensory data, deciding when to speed up, slow down, or swerve to avoid hitting an object or person. The AI in these cars must understand the rules of the road, the vehicle's capabilities, and the dynamic environment around them. This decision-making process involves a level of reasoning that's quite sophisticated—analyzing the current situation, predicting potential outcomes, and making decisions that avoid accidents and ensure passenger safety.

Yet, despite these advances, AI technologies are limited in mimicking human intelligence. One of the biggest challenges is understanding context and nuance. Humans are exceptionally good at this. We pick up on subtle cues in conversation, understand sarcasm, and can navigate complex social interactions. AI, however, can struggle here. It might misinterpret the meaning of a text based on missing contextual cues or fail to recognize the emotional undertones in a conversation. This limitation indicates a significant gap between human cognitive abilities and current AI capabilities. It reminds us that while AI can learn and reason, it doesn't "understand" as humans do.

The ethical implications of AI systems that mimic human behaviors are profound and multifaceted. As AI becomes more integrated into our daily lives, issues of privacy and autonomy come to the forefront. Consider smart home assistants that listen to our conversations to better anticipate our needs. While convenient, they also raise concerns about surveillance and data privacy. Who is listening, and what happens to our data? Then there's the question of autonomy. As decision-making processes become more automated, at what point do we lose our agency in making choices about our lives? These are not just technical questions but deeply ethical ones, challenging us to consider how we balance the benefits of AI with the preservation of fundamental human rights.

Understanding these facets of AI helps us understand the technology and encourages a more informed conversation about its role in our future. It's not just about marveling at what AI can do but also questioning and critically examining how it does these things and at what cost. As we continue to develop and deploy AI technologies, keeping these considerations in mind ensures that we remain thoughtful about shaping a world where humans and machines coexist.

1.4 Machine Learning Simplified: AI's Learning Process

Have you ever watched a toddler learn to recognize and name animals? First, you show them a picture of a dog and say "dog," then a cat and say "cat." Over time, they start pointing at dogs in books and barking, and you know they've got it. Machine learning works astonishingly similarly, but instead of animal pictures, it uses data and lots of it. At its core, machine learning is the process by which computers learn from data to make decisions and predictions without being explicitly programmed for each task.

Let's break this down a bit. Traditionally, to make a computer perform a task, you'd write a detailed set of instructions (a program) in a computer language. However, with machine learning, the computer develops its own program based on examples. This capability is why machine learning is often seen as the backbone of AI—it enables machines to make decisions and improve over time, much like humans do, but at a scale and speed that is just mind-boggling.

There are two main types of machine learning: supervised and unsupervised. Think of supervised learning as learning with a guide. You provide the machine learning model with labeled examples. Suppose you're teaching it to differentiate between spam and non-spam emails. In that case, you'll provide it with thousands of emails that are already marked as 'spam' or 'not spam.' The model uses these examples to learn how to classify future emails.

With unsupervised learning, you let the model sift through data and find patterns on its own. Imagine dumping a box of colored balls in front of a child and letting them organize the balls without instructions. They could decide to sort them by color, size, or even by how much they bounce. Similarly, unsupervised learning algorithms find all sorts of connections in data that might not be immediately apparent to human observers.

Both these methods have fascinating applications that touch everything from your daily shopping to securing your personal data. Take recommendation systems, for instance. Have you ever wondered how Spotify seems to know your music taste? Well, it uses unsupervised learning to find patterns in the types of songs you listen to and then makes predictions about what other songs you might like. An example of supervised learning is credit card fraud detection. Here, supervised learning models look at transactions that are known to be fraudulent and learn to flag similar transactions in the future.

As we peer into the future of machine learning, the possibilities start to get even more exhilarating (and a bit sci-fi). We're looking at advancements that could allow machines to learn from much smaller data sets called "few-shot learning," which mimics how humans can often learn from very few examples. Imagine teaching a machine learning model to recognize a new type of scam email from just a handful of examples. This advancement could significantly reduce the data needed to train effective models, making machine learning even more accessible across different fields.

In the grand tapestry of AI, machine learning is not just a thread but a crucial pattern weaving through the entire design, continually expanding in complexity and capability. As these technologies advance, they promise to unlock new potentials, foster unseen innovations, and perhaps, most importantly, work alongside us to tackle some of the most pressing challenges we face today. Whether fighting climate change, improving healthcare, or securing our data, machine learning stands at the forefront, ready to transform vast data landscapes into actionable insights and intelligent actions.

1.5 Demystifying Deep Learning: Neural Networks Explained

Imagine you're at a bustling party, trying to pick out the different conversations around you. Your brain effortlessly focuses on various sounds, identifies voices, and filters out irrelevant noise. This incredible ability of your brain to process complex information is what inspired the creation of neural networks in deep learning. In short, neural networks are a set of algorithms. They aren't identical to, but are modeled after this working of the human brain responsible for recognizing patterns. These networks interpret sensory data by sorting and grouping the raw information they receive. The basic building blocks of these networks are neurons—tiny data processors that are connected together and work in unison to solve specific problems.

So, in a nutshell, these neural networks consist of layers upon layers of interconnected neurons. More specifically, they will have an input layer, one or more hidden layers, and an output layer. The magic happens in the hidden layers, where the processing and pattern recognition occur. Each neuron in a layer is connected to several others in the next layer. As data travels through the layers, each neuron assigns a weighting to its input—how important it is relative to other inputs—before passing it on. Through training, these networks adjust these weights based on the accuracy of their outcomes, continually learning and improving their performance.

Deep learning comes into play when these neural networks have multiple (deep) hidden layers, which allow them to model complex phenomena such as speech and image recognition. To see this in action, think about when you upload photos to a social media site, and it automatically tags your friends. This is deep learning at work—algorithms processing vast amounts of data (all the tagged photos it has seen before) to recognize and learn faces.

However, training deep learning models isn't a walk in the park. They require substantial computational power and massive datasets, which are not always readily available or easy to compile. The models must be trained on thousands, if not millions, of examples to perform well. This training can be resource-intensive, requiring powerful GPUs (Graphics Processing Units)* and significant energy, which brings us to some practical challenges in deep learning. The sheer volume of data needed can lead to longer training times and the necessity of specialized hardware, which can be expensive and not accessible for many.

Then there are the ethical considerations. As powerful as deep learning is, it's not immune to biases, especially if the data it's trained on is skewed. For example, suppose a facial recognition system is trained primarily on images of people from one ethnic group. In that case, it might not perform as well with pictures of people from other backgrounds. This bias can lead to fairness issues, where particular groups receive less accurate or fair treatment by systems that use these technologies. Transparency is another ethical challenge. Deep learning models, particularly those with many layers, can become "black boxes," where even their designers struggle to explain how exactly they arrived at certain decisions. This gap in transparency can be problematic, especially in sensitive applications such as medical diagnosis or in judicial systems where understanding the basis of a decision is essential.

Deploying deep learning systems thus brings a host of ethical dilemmas that we must navigate carefully. Ensuring these systems are fair and their workings transparent requires ongoing effort and vigilance from developers, regulators, and users alike. As we integrate these advanced technologies into more aspects of our lives, the responsibility grows to guard against their potential to perpetuate or amplify biases inadvertently. This dual challenge of pushing technological boundaries while safeguarding ethical standards is central to the future of deep learning.

In embracing these technologies, we are tasked with balancing innovation with responsibility—a theme that reoccurs throughout the development and application of AI. As deep learning continues to evolve, it promises new possibilities and solutions but also poses new questions and challenges, reminding us that progress in AI, like all advancements, is as much about the questions we ask and the limits we set as it is about the capabilities we develop.

1.6 AI Ethics: Balancing Innovation with Responsibility

With this superpower at our fingertips, it needs to be repeated that with great power comes great responsibility. This guiding principle is particularly apt when we talk about the development and use of Artificial Intelligence. As we integrate AI more deeply into our daily lives and global infrastructure, it's crucial to steer this powerful technology responsibly. This approach isn't just about preventing robots from taking over the world; it's about ensuring that AI improves lives without infringing on rights or exacerbating inequalities.

Ethical AI isn't just a nice-to-have; it's a must-have, and here's why: technologies reflect the values of those who create them. Without careful consideration, AI can perpetuate biases, invade privacy, and even unintentionally cause harm. For instance, think about a job application screening tool. Suppose it's trained primarily on successful resumes from a demographic that doesn't include women or minorities. In that case, it may inadvertently favor candidates who fit a particular profile, thus perpetuating existing biases. Similarly, AI-powered surveillance tools could invade privacy if used without clear ethical guidelines. The implications are vast and varied, affecting everything from job prospects to personal freedoms.

So, what are the key ethical concerns we should be aware of? Bias, as mentioned, is a big one. Then there's privacy—ensuring that AI systems respect user data and don't become tools for unwarranted surveillance. Job displacement is another critical issue. As AI automates tasks, what happens to the people whose livelihoods depend on those tasks? These are societal challenges touching every facet of our existence that require thoughtful solutions considering the broader human context.

Thankfully, we're not navigating these waters without a compass. There are existing frameworks and guidelines designed to help developers and users ensure AI is used ethically. For example, the EU's Ethics Guidelines for Trustworthy AI is a robust framework that outlines requirements like transparency, accountability, and fairness. These guidelines encourage developers to create lawful, ethical, and robust AI, standing up to scrutiny while respecting human rights. Similarly, IEEE's (Institute for Electrical and Electronics Engineers) *Ethically Aligned Design* provides a set of principles that prioritize human well-being in AI systems. These frameworks aren't just about preventing misuse but proactively guiding AI development to benefit humanity universally.

But here's the kicker: no framework or guideline can enforce itself. That's where the irreplaceable role of humans in AI ethics comes into play. It's up to us—developers, users, policymakers—to ensure these principles are followed. This means designing

AI with ethical considerations in mind from the start and maintaining diligent oversight throughout an AI system's life cycle. For instance, regular audits of AI applications in high-stakes areas like healthcare and law enforcement can help ensure they perform as intended without causing harm.

Moreover, transparency is vital. This doesn't just mean making the code available (which can be indecipherable to the everyday human) but also providing clear, understandable explanations of how AI systems make decisions. This kind of transparency builds trust and allows for informed consent from users, who deserve to understand how technologies might affect their lives.

Accountability mechanisms are equally important. When something goes wrong—as it inevitably will at some point—who is responsible? Is it the developers, the company deploying the AI, or the algorithms themselves? Establishing clear lines of accountability ensures that AI is used responsibly and that there are remedies when things go astray. Examples are setting up regulatory bodies specifically for AI or incorporating AI ethics into existing oversight structures.

Navigating AI ethics is like setting rules for a new game. Everyone needs to understand the rules, agree to follow them, and be clear about the consequences of breaking them. This approach doesn't stifle innovation but guides it along a path that maximizes benefits while minimizing harm. As we continue to unleash the transformative potential of AI, let's commit to harnessing this technology not just with our ingenuity but also with our values. After all, technology is at its best when used to lift everyone up, not as a wedge driving us apart.

As we move forward with integrating AI into the fabric of society, let's remember that every line of code can carry the weight of ethical implications. We must ensure that these digital decisions make our world fairer, safer, and more equitable. It's not just about what AI can do but what it should do. Ultimately, the goal is to create AI that works efficiently and aligns closely with the ethical values we hold dear, ensuring that the future we're building is one we can all look forward to.

Chapter 2

Overcoming Challenges in AI Learning

W hen you first enter the world of AI, it can feel overwhelming, as if everyone else received a secret memo on how to speak this complex technical language while you were busy hitting the snooze button. But don't worry! This chapter is here to translate all that tech-speak into plain English. We'll break down the jargon, decode the acronyms, and make AI as easy to understand as your favorite recipe.

Normally, you would find the glossary at the end of the book you are reading, so starting Chapter 2 with this might seem odd. However, there is a very good reason for the glossary to be here. Learning AI is, in part, also learning a new language. Without understanding terms such as Deep Learning or acronyms such as IoT (Internet of Things), it is going to be next to impossible for you to start building confidence in this field. Tedious as it might seem, take your time going through the glossary and refer back to it when reading through the book and you come across one of them. You will thank yourself in the end!

2.1 Breaking Down AI Jargon: A Glossary for Beginners

Let's get you speaking some basic AI. Here are a few terms that appear frequently in AI discussions:

Glossary

A

- Algorithm: A set of step-by-step instructions for solving problems or performing tasks in AI.

  - Example: Algorithms are like recipes that AI systems follow to make decisions or predictions based on input data.

- Application Programming Interface (API): A set of rules, protocols, and tools that specify how software components should interact with each other. APIs define the kinds of requests that can be made, how to make them, the data formats that should be used, and the conventions to follow. In the context of AI, APIs allow developers to integrate AI capabilities, such as machine learning or natural language processing, into their applications without building the underlying models from scratch.

  - Example: The Google Cloud Vision API enables developers to incorporate image recognition and analysis capabilities into their applications without needing to develop complex computer vision models themselves.

- Artificial Intelligence (AI): The field of computer science that focuses on creating intelligent machines that can perform tasks that typically require human intelligence.

  - Example: Virtual assistants like Siri or Alexa use AI to understand and respond to voice commands.

B

- Backpropagation: An algorithm used in training neural networks to calculate the gradient of the loss function with respect to the weights of the network.

- Example: Backpropagation allows the error to be propagated backward through the layers of the neural network, enabling the weights to be updated.

- BERT (Bidirectional Encoder Representations from Transformers): A pre-trained deep learning model developed by Google for natural language processing tasks. BERT is designed to understand the context and meaning of words in a sentence by considering the words that come before and after each word.

  - Example: BERT can be fine-tuned for various NLP tasks, such as sentiment analysis or question answering, allowing developers to leverage its pre-trained knowledge and achieve high accuracy with relatively small amounts of task-specific training data.

- Big Data: Extremely large datasets that may be analyzed computationally to reveal patterns, trends, and associations, especially relating to human behavior and interactions. Big data often requires specialized tools and techniques for storage, processing, and analysis, such as distributed computing and parallel processing.

  - Example: Social media platforms generate vast amounts of big data, which can be analyzed to understand user preferences, sentiment, and social trends.

C

- Central Processing Unit (CPU): The primary component of a computer that processes instructions and performs calculations. CPUs are versatile but may be slower than GPUs for certain tasks in machine learning.

  - Example: CPUs are used for general-purpose computing tasks and can be used for inference (making predictions) with trained machine learning models.

- Chatbot: A computer program or an artificial intelligence that conducts a conversation via auditory or textual methods. Chatbots are commonly used in customer service, information retrieval, and entertainment applications.

  - Example: A customer service chatbot can handle common inquiries, such as order status or product information, freeing up human agents to handle more complex issues.

- Computer Vision (CV): The field of AI that focuses on enabling computers to interpret and understand visual information from the world.

  - Example: CV is used in autonomous vehicles to detect and recognize objects, pedestrians, and road signs.

- Convolutional Neural Network (CNN): A type of neural network commonly used in image recognition and computer vision tasks.

  - Example: CNNs are used in facial recognition systems to detect and identify individuals from images or video feeds.

D

- Data Preprocessing: The process of cleaning, transforming, and preparing raw data for use in machine learning algorithms.

  - Example: Data preprocessing tasks include removing duplicate or irrelevant data, handling missing values, and normalizing numeric features.

- Data Science: An interdisciplinary field that uses scientific methods, processes, algorithms, and systems to extract knowledge and insights from structured and unstructured data. Data science encompasses a broad range of techniques and tools used in machine learning, data analysis, and data visualization.

  - Example: Data science techniques can be applied to analyze user behavior on an e-commerce website, identifying patterns and trends that can inform marketing strategies and product recommendations.

- Decision Trees: A type of machine learning algorithm that creates a tree-like model of decisions and their possible consequences. Decision trees are used for both classification and regression tasks.

  - Example: A decision tree for predicting whether a customer will buy a product based on their age and income might have branches like "If age < 30 and income < \$50,000, then predict 'No'; else if age >= 30 and income >= \$50,000, then predict 'Yes'."

- Deep Learning (DL): A subfield of machine learning that uses artificial neural networks with multiple layers to learn from vast amounts of data.

    ○ Example: Deep learning is used in image recognition systems, such as those that can identify objects or faces in photos.

- Dynamic computational graph: Often associated with deep learning frameworks like PyTorch, dynamic computational graphs are flexible and adaptive systems that build the computational graph on the fly as operations are executed. This contrasts with static computational graphs, which are defined and fixed before the computation starts.

    ○ Example: Teaching a computer to predict the next word in a sentence. A dynamic computational graph allows the model to adapt to each sentence's length as it processes them. This means that each time a new sentence is input, the computer creates a unique pathway to handle the specific length and structure of that sentence. This flexibility makes it easier to work with real-world data, where inputs often vary in size and shape.

E

- Explainable AI (XAI): A set of techniques and methods aimed at making AI systems more transparent and interpretable, enabling users to understand how decisions are made.

    ○ Example: XAI techniques can be used to highlight the specific features or patterns that influenced a model's prediction, making the decision-making process more transparent.

F

- Feature Extraction: The process of selecting or transforming variables (features) from raw data to improve the performance of machine learning models.

    ○ Example: In text classification, feature extraction might involve converting words into numerical representations, such as word embeddings or TF-IDF vectors.

G

- Generative Adversarial Network (GAN): A type of deep learning model that consists of two neural networks, a generator and a discriminator, which compete against each other to generate new, synthetic data that resembles the training data.

- Example: GANs can be used to generate realistic images, such as creating artificial faces that look similar to real human faces, or to generate new designs for products like fashion items or furniture.

- Generative Pre-trained Transformer (GPT): A series of language models developed by OpenAI that use unsupervised learning to generate human-like text. GPT models, such as GPT-4, have been used in various applications, including chatbots, content generation, and code completion.

- Example: GPT-4 can be used to generate realistic text snippets, such as news articles or creative writing, based on a given prompt or context.

- Gradient Descent: An optimization algorithm commonly used in machine learning to minimize a cost function by iteratively adjusting the parameters of a model.

- Example: Gradient descent is used in training neural networks to update the weights and biases in the direction that minimizes the prediction error.

- Graphics Processing Unit (GPU): A specialized electronic circuit designed to rapidly manipulate and alter memory to accelerate the creation of images in a frame buffer intended for output to a display device. GPUs are commonly used in training deep learning models due to their ability to perform parallel computations efficiently.

- Example: GPUs are used to accelerate the training of large neural networks, reducing the time required to train models on vast amounts of data.

H

- Hyperparameters: The settings or configuration variables that are set before training a machine learning model. These parameters control the behavior of the learning algorithm and can be tuned to optimize the model's performance.

- Example: The learning rate, which determines how much the model's weights are adjusted during training, is a common hyperparameter in neural networks.

I

- Integrated Development Environment (IDE): A software application that provides comprehensive facilities to computer programmers for software development. IDEs typically include features such as a source code editor, build automation tools, and a debugger. Popular IDEs for AI development include Jupyter Notebook, PyCharm, and Visual Studio Code.

  ○ Example: Jupyter Notebook is an IDE that allows developers to create and share documents containing live code, equations, visualizations, and narrative text, making it popular for data science and machine learning projects.

- Internet of Things (IoT): A network of physical devices, vehicles, home appliances, and other items embedded with electronics, software, sensors, and network connectivity, enabling these objects to collect and exchange data. IoT devices can be controlled and monitored remotely, allowing for automation and efficient management of various systems.

  ○ Example: A smart thermostat that learns your temperature preferences and automatically adjusts your home's heating and cooling based on your daily routines is an example of an IoT device.

J

*

K

- K Clusters: In the context of the K-means clustering algorithm, K represents the number of clusters or groups into which the data points are divided. The algorithm aims to partition n observations into K clusters, where each observation belongs to the cluster with the nearest mean.

  ○ Example: If you have a dataset of customer purchase histories and you want to divide them into 5 segments based on their buying behavior, you would set K = 5 in the K-means algorithm.

- Keras: An open-source neural network library written in Python that can run on top of TensorFlow, Microsoft Cognitive Toolkit, R, Theano, or PlaidML. Keras is designed to enable fast experimentation with deep neural networks and focuses on being user-friendly, modular, and extensible.

- ○ Example: Keras provides a high-level, user-friendly interface for building and training deep learning models, making it easier for beginners to get started with neural networks.

L

- Long Short-Term Memory (LSTM): A type of recurrent neural network architecture that is capable of learning long-term dependencies. LSTMs are commonly used in tasks such as speech recognition, language translation, and text generation.

  - ○ Example: LSTMs are used in speech recognition systems to process and recognize spoken words, taking into account the context and long-term dependencies in the audio data.

M

- Machine Learning (ML): A subset of AI that involves training algorithms to learn patterns from data and make predictions or decisions without being explicitly programmed.

  - ○ Example: Email spam filters use machine learning to identify and separate unwanted emails based on patterns learned from previous examples.

- matplotlib: A Python library used for creating static, animated, and interactive visualizations. Matplotlib provides a wide range of functionalities for creating various types of plots, charts, and graphs.

  - ○ Example: You can use matplotlib to create line plots, scatter plots, bar charts, histograms, and more, making it a versatile tool for visualizing data in machine learning and data science projects.

N

- N Observations: In machine learning, N refers to the number of data points or samples in a dataset. Each observation represents a single instance of the data, such as a customer transaction, a sensor reading, or a medical record.

- Example: If you have a dataset containing information about 1,000 customers, then N = 1,000, and each customer's data is considered a single observation.

- Natural Language Processing (NLP): The ability of a computer program to understand, interpret, and generate human language.

  ○ Example: NLP is used in language translation apps like Google Translate to convert text from one language to another.

- Neural Network: A set of algorithms modeled loosely after the human brain, designed to recognize patterns and learn from data.

  ○ Example: Neural networks process data from cameras and sensors in self-driving cars to make real-time driving decisions.

- NumPy: A Python library used for numerical computing. NumPy provides support for large, multi-dimensional arrays and matrices, along with a collection of mathematical functions to operate on these arrays efficiently.

  ○ Example: NumPy is often used in machine learning projects to perform operations on large datasets, such as computing the mean, standard deviation, or matrix multiplication of arrays.

O

- Overfitting: A common problem in machine learning where a model learns the noise in the training data to the extent that it negatively impacts its performance on new data.

  ○ Example: An overfitted model might perform well on the training data but fail to generalize to new, unseen data.

P

- Parsing: The process of analyzing a string of symbols or tokens conforming to the rules of a formal grammar. In natural language processing, parsing involves analyzing the grammatical structure of a sentence to determine its meaning.

  ○ Example: A parser can break down a sentence like "The quick brown fox jumps over the lazy dog" into its constituent parts of speech (noun, verb, adjective) and identify the subject, verb, and object of the sentence.

- PyTorch: An open-source machine learning library based on the Torch library, primarily developed by Facebook's AI Research lab. PyTorch is known for its dynamic computational graph and ease of use, making it popular among researchers and developers.

- o Example: PyTorch is often used in research settings to quickly prototype and experiment with new neural network architectures and training techniques.

Q

*

R

- Random Forests: An ensemble learning method for classification, regression, and other tasks that operate by constructing a multitude of decision trees at training time and outputting the class that is the mode of the classes (classification) or mean prediction (regression) of the individual trees.

  - o Example: Random forests can be used for tasks such as predicting whether a customer will churn or not based on their demographic information and usage patterns.

- Recurrent Neural Network (RNN): A type of neural network designed to handle sequential data, such as time series or natural language.

  - o Example: RNNs are used in language modeling tasks, such as predicting the next word in a sentence based on the previous words.

- Reinforcement Learning: A type of machine learning where an agent learns to make decisions by interacting with an environment and receiving rewards or punishments.

  - o Example: Reinforcement learning is used in gaming AI, where the algorithm learns to make optimal moves based on the game state and rewards (e.g., winning or losing).

S

- SciPy: A Python library used for scientific and technical computing. SciPy builds on NumPy and provides additional functions for optimization, linear algebra, integration, interpolation, signal and image processing, statistics, and more.

  - o Example: SciPy can be used in machine learning projects for tasks such as optimization of model parameters, signal processing, or statistical analysis of results.

- Scikit-learn (sklearn): A free software machine learning library for the Python programming language. Scikit-learn provides a wide range of supervised and unsupervised learning algorithms and is built on top of NumPy, SciPy, and matplotlib.

  - Example: Scikit-learn can be used to quickly train and evaluate various machine learning models, such as decision trees, support vector machines, and random forests, on structured data.

- Semantic Reasoning: The process of understanding the meaning of words, phrases, and sentences in context. In natural language processing, semantic reasoning involves using machine learning techniques to infer the intended meaning of text based on the relationships between words and their contexts.

  - Example: A semantic reasoning system could infer that the phrase "I'm feeling blue" refers to a person's emotional state (sadness) rather than the color blue.

- Software Development Kit (SDK): A collection of software development tools, libraries, documentation, and code samples that allows developers to create applications for a specific platform or programming language. Many AI platforms provide SDKs to simplify the integration of AI capabilities into applications.

  - Example: The TensorFlow SDK provides tools and libraries for developing and deploying machine learning models in various programming languages.

- Stemming: The process of reducing words to their base or root form. Stemming is a common preprocessing step in natural language processing that helps reduce the dimensionality of the text data by treating different forms of the same word as a single entity.

  - Example: The words "running," "runs," and "ran" would all be reduced to the base form "run" by a stemming algorithm.

- Supervised Learning: A type of machine learning where the algorithm learns from labeled data with input-output pairs.

- o Example: A supervised learning algorithm can be trained on a dataset of labeled images (e.g., "cat" or "dog") to classify new, unlabeled images.

- Support Vector Machines (SVM): A type of supervised learning algorithm used for classification, regression, and outlier detection tasks. SVMs aim to find the hyperplane that best separates the different classes in the feature space while maximizing the margin between the classes.

  - o Example: SVMs can be used for tasks such as classifying emails as spam or not spam based on the content and metadata of the emails.

T

- TensorFlow: An open-source software library for machine learning developed by Google. TensorFlow provides a comprehensive ecosystem of tools, libraries, and resources for building and deploying ML models.

  - o Example: TensorFlow can be used to build and train deep neural networks for various tasks, such as image classification, natural language processing, and recommendation systems.

- Tokenization: The process of breaking down a piece of text into smaller units called tokens. Tokens can be individual words, phrases, or even whole sentences. Tokenization is a fundamental step in natural language processing that helps prepare the text data for further analysis.

  - o Example: The sentence "I love artificial intelligence!" could be tokenized into the individual words: "I," "love," "artificial," "intelligence," and "!".

- Transformer: A type of neural network architecture that is particularly effective at processing sequential data, such as text. Transformers can understand the context and relationships between words in a sentence, making them useful for tasks involving natural language.

  - o Example: A Transformer-based model can be used to improve the accuracy of language translation. For instance, when translating the sentence "I'm excited to visit my grandparents" from English to Spanish, the Transformer model would consider the context and meaning of each word to provide a more accurate translation, such as "Estoy emocionado de visitar a mis abuelos," rather than translating each word individually.

- Transfer Learning: A technique in machine learning where knowledge gained from solving one problem is applied to a different but related problem.

   ○ Example: A neural network trained on a large dataset of images can be fine-tuned for a specific task, like detecting medical abnormalities in X-rays, using a smaller dataset.

U

• Underfitting: A situation in machine learning where a model is too simple to capture the underlying patterns in the data.

   ○ Example: An underfit model might perform poorly on both the training data and new data, failing to learn the relevant patterns.

• Unsupervised Learning: A type of machine learning where the algorithm learns from unlabeled data, discovering hidden patterns or structures.

   ○ Example: Unsupervised learning can be used to cluster customers based on their purchasing

V, W, X, Y, Z

*

The language of AI is constantly evolving. New terms and technologies emerge as quickly as new social media trends. Keeping up might seem daunting, but it's all about staying curious and continuously learning. This can be as simple as following AI blogs, joining online communities, or listening to AI podcasts. The key is to make learning a habit, something you do a little bit of every day.

Make sure you bookmark this page. You will want to come back to it as you work your way through the book.

2.2 Overcoming the "Too Late to Start" Mentality in AI Learning

You might think you've missed the AI train because you didn't start coding as a child or weren't part of the smartphone generation from day one. However, starting your AI learning journey later in life isn't just possible; it can be a significant advantage. The world of AI is diverse, and your unique experiences and perspectives are valuable assets. Let's tackle those doubts and show you how the "too late" myth is just that—a myth.

First, let's address a common fear: "I'm too old to learn something as complex as AI." AI isn't just for young tech prodigies. It's for anyone with curiosity and a willingness to learn. Remember, AI is about solving problems, and who better to tackle these than someone with more life experience?

Another concern is the belief that you need a background in tech or data science. While those can help, they're not prerequisites. Many successful AI practitioners come from diverse fields—arts, medicine, journalism, and more. They bring their unique perspectives to the table, enriching the AI landscape.

Consider the story of Linda, a former teacher who started learning AI at 58. She used her new skills to develop an AI program that helps identify students' learning gaps. Or Jim, who retired from his construction business and took up AI as a hobby. He's now working on an AI tool to optimize material usage on construction sites. These stories demonstrate that AI learning has no age limit.

If you're ready to dive into AI, start small. Online courses tailored for beginners can be a great entry point. Look for courses that focus on AI fundamentals and gradually progress to more advanced topics. AI learning apps and interactive web platforms also offer hands-on practice without overwhelming you.

Another excellent option is to join community classes or workshops. These often provide a more relaxed learning environment and the opportunity to learn alongside others who are also starting their AI journey.

Remember, the world of AI benefits immensely from diverse ideas and experiences. Every new learner brings a fresh perspective that can lead to innovative solutions. Your background, whatever it may be, provides you with a unique lens through which to understand and apply AI concepts.

Give yourself credit for even considering stepping into the world of AI. It's a field that's transforming the world and constantly evolving, which means it's always looking for fresh ideas and new perspectives. Your journey into AI might just be the key to unlocking innovations we've barely begun to imagine.

As you continue exploring AI, remember that every expert was once a beginner. The only thing that set them apart was their willingness to start and their persistence to keep going. Whether you're looking to switch careers, enhance your current job, or simply satisfy your curiosity about AI, now is the perfect time to get started. Embrace your unique insights, harness your life experiences, and let them guide you on your AI learning path.

2.3 AI Ethics: Understanding Bias and Fairness

AI systems, like sponges, soak up whatever data they are trained on, absorbing the good, the bad, and the biased. If the data used to train an AI model is biased, the AI's decisions will reflect those biases. This can lead to unfair outcomes and skewed decision-making, affecting everything from job applicant screenings to loan approvals.

For example, if an AI hiring system is trained primarily on resumes of successful candidates from a specific demographic, it may inadvertently favor applicants who fit that profile, perpetuating existing biases. This isn't because the AI has a personal agenda; it's merely mirroring the biases present in its training data. Fairness takes a hit when AI reinforces biased patterns instead of providing equal opportunities.

The ethical implications are significant, spanning ethical, social, and legal domains. It's not just about ensuring the technology functions correctly; it's about making sure it upholds values like fairness and equality.

One strategy to mitigate these biases is to ensure diversity in the data used to train AI models. Just as a balanced diet keeps you healthy, a diverse dataset helps keep AI fair. This means gathering data from a wide range of sources and perspectives to provide the AI with a comprehensive view.

Continuous monitoring is another crucial tactic. Regularly auditing AI systems can help identify biases early on, allowing for timely adjustments. It's about maintaining a watchful eye to make sure the AI stays on track.

Transparency is also key. When AI systems are like black boxes, with their internal workings hidden, it's challenging to identify where things go wrong. Making these systems transparent by providing clear explanations of how decisions are made helps build trust and accountability.

Ethical frameworks and guidelines play a vital role in shaping the development and use of AI. Organizations like the AI Now Institute and initiatives like the Montreal Declaration for Responsible AI are working to establish guidelines that cover aspects like ensuring AI respects human rights, promotes inclusivity, and prevents harm. Following these guidelines helps ensure that AI is developed and deployed in a manner that prioritizes ethical considerations alongside technical advancements.

However, guidelines alone are not enough. Developers, users, and policymakers must ensure these principles are put into practice. This means designing AI with ethical considerations from the start, regularly auditing systems for biases, and maintaining transparency in how AI makes decisions.

In one case, an AI hiring system was found to be biased against women due to imbalances in its training data, which featured a higher proportion of successful male candidates. As a result, qualified women were overlooked, perpetuating gender bias in the workplace.

Addressing AI bias is more than tweaking algorithms; it's about setting new standards for how we develop, deploy, and manage AI. It's about ensuring that as we embrace this powerful technology, we're taking everyone along, providing every individual with a fair chance to benefit from AI's potential. By tackling AI bias head-on, we're making this technology fairer and our society more just and equitable.

As we continue to explore the ethical landscape of AI, remember that it's not just about avoiding pitfalls; it's about actively shaping AI to improve lives without exacerbating inequalities. Every step we take towards ethical AI is a stride towards a future where technology and humanity coexist in a fairer, more inclusive world.

2.4 From Concept to Application: Translating AI Knowledge into Action

Learning about AI concepts is one thing, but applying that knowledge to real-world projects is where the true magic happens. It's the difference between reading a recipe and actually baking the cake. Translating AI knowledge into practical applications might seem daunting, but it's a crucial step in cementing your understanding and developing valuable skills.

Navigating from theory to practice can be challenging, but starting small is key. You don't need to build a complex AI system right off the bat. Begin with bite-sized projects that align with your interests or professional needs. If you're in marketing, try using AI tools to analyze consumer data and personalize ads. If you're a photography enthusiast, experiment with AI-powered photo editing software. The goal is to apply AI in ways that complement and enhance your existing skills and passions, turning abstract concepts into tangible tools.

Project-based learning is an effective approach to reinforce your AI knowledge. This involves tackling specific, practical projects that apply AI principles. It's a hands-on method where you start with a goal, like automating appointment scheduling, and then break down the steps to achieve it, from selecting the right tools to programming the AI. This approach not only helps solidify your understanding but also gives you practical experience in applying AI to solve real-world problems.

Finding opportunities to apply AI might seem tricky, especially if you're not in a tech-centric profession. However, AI's versatility means it can be applied in fields ranging from agriculture to art. Start by identifying processes in your daily life or job that AI could optimize. It could be analyzing financial trends to better advise clients or automating data entry tasks. You can also look to your local community—schools, small businesses, non-profits—and consider how AI might solve common challenges they face. Even volunteering your burgeoning AI skills can provide valuable hands-on experience while making a positive impact.

Documenting and sharing your AI projects is crucial for your growth. Think of it as keeping a learning journal where you track your progress, challenges, and achievements. Maintaining a blog or online portfolio can be an excellent way to showcase your work. Share your successes and setbacks. It's not just about building a personal archive but also about contributing to the broader AI community. Peer feedback can provide new insights and help refine your approach while sharing your experiences can guide and inspire others on their AI journey. Platforms like GitHub or AI-focused social media groups can be perfect for this kind of exchange.

Remember, diving into AI applications is less about having all the answers before you start and more about being willing to learn and adapt as you go. Every project will teach you something new, not just about AI but also about problem-solving and creative thinking. Embrace the challenges, celebrate your progress, and let every project, no matter how small, be a stepping stone in your AI adventure.

By actively applying your AI knowledge, you're not just a bystander in the world of tech—you're a participant, shaping your own path and potentially paving the way for others to follow. So, roll up your sleeves, dive into a project, and watch as the concepts you've learned come to life in exciting, impactful ways.

2.5 Building Confidence: Overcoming Fear of Technical Complexity

When you first peek into the world of AI, it can seem like you are staring up at a towering mountain of codes, algorithms, and data models. Feeling overwhelmed or doubting your ability to climb this technical mountain is completely normal. But remember, every seasoned climber started with a single step, and every AI expert began with the basics.

Incremental learning is a time-tested strategy for managing complex subjects. Start with the fundamentals of AI—what it is and how it works at a basic level. Focus on grasping simple concepts before moving on to more intricate topics. This approach is similar to learning a new language; you begin with common phrases and everyday vocabulary before tackling complex literature.

Online platforms offer AI courses structured to guide you from basics to advanced concepts at a pace that suits you. They often include interactive elements like quizzes or coding exercises that reinforce your understanding and give you a sense of progress. Celebrating these small victories is both fun and important. Completing a module, writing your first lines of code, or running your first successful AI model—these are all milestones worth acknowledging. Recognizing these achievements, no matter how small they might seem, builds your confidence and motivation.

Seeking support is essential in transforming AI from a daunting subject into a manageable one. Join study groups or online communities where you can exchange ideas, ask questions, and share resources. These communities provide both technical support and moral encouragement. AI isn't a solo journey; it's a field built on collaboration and shared knowledge. Engaging with others can offer new insights and approaches you might not have considered. Platforms like Meetup often host AI learning groups, and online forums like Stack Overflow are goldmines for support and advice. Mentorship can also be invaluable. A mentor in AI can guide you through complex concepts and offer tailored advice based on their experience.

As you continue to learn and engage with AI, remember that every expert you encounter, every professional you admire in this field, once stood where you stand now. They faced the same complexities and the same steep learning curve, and they moved forward—one step at a time, just as you are doing now.

Keep learning, keep questioning, and keep climbing that mountain. With each new concept mastered and each challenge overcome, you're not just learning AI; you're mastering the art of learning itself, which is perhaps the most valuable skill in today's ever-evolving technological landscape.

2.6 Finding Your AI Learning Path: Resources and Roadmaps

Navigating the AI learning landscape can feel like choosing a path in a dense forest. Think of it as sketching out a trail map that can adapt as you discover new AI territories you want to explore, forging a learning path that aligns with your personal interests, skill level, and goals.

Creating a personalized AI learning path starts with self-reflection. What excites you about AI? Is it the potential to solve complex puzzles or the opportunity to integrate AI into your current career? You may be fascinated by AI ethics or keen to explore how AI can enhance healthcare. Identifying these interests helps anchor your learning path.

Next, assess your current skill level. Are you a complete beginner, or do you have some tech experience? Finally, define your goals. Are you aiming to shift careers entirely, enhance your current job with AI skills, or explore AI out of curiosity?

You can start building your path once you have a clear picture of these elements. Begin with foundational courses if you're a beginner or more specialized classes if you have some experience. Incorporate a mix of theoretical learning and practical application—this could mean online courses coupled with hands-on projects. Don't forget to sprinkle in some soft skills like problem-solving and critical thinking, which are just as crucial in AI as technical abilities.

For those just starting out, platforms like Coursera and Udemy offer a wide range of AI courses tailored for beginners. More advanced learners might find platforms like edX and Fast.ai beneficial for deeper dives into complex AI topics. Don't overlook the wealth of knowledge available in AI research papers on sites like arXiv.org, which can give you a glimpse into cutting-edge advancements.

Podcasts like "1" or "2" and blogs by AI thought leaders or organizations like OpenAI and DeepMind can also be invaluable. These resources keep you updated on the latest AI trends and discussions, sparking ideas and inspiring projects. For hands-on learners, Kaggle offers AI competitions and datasets that allow you to test and refine your skills in real-world scenarios.

Setting achievable goals is about understanding what's feasible in the short and long term. It's about breaking down your ultimate AI vision into manageable, bite-sized pieces. Start by setting small, weekly goals—maybe completing one module of an online course or reading one AI article every day. Celebrate these small victories; they add up and keep your motivation burning. Gradually, these smaller goals will lead you towards more significant achievements.

Like any exciting adventure, your AI learning path might need some rerouting as you progress. New interests might emerge, or specific areas may resonate less than you initially thought. Regularly take stock of your progress and interests. You may have started out fascinated by machine learning but have found a growing interest in AI ethics. Shift your learning resources and projects to include these new interests. The key is to stay flexible and open to where the AI path might lead you.

Embrace this dynamic journey with an open mind and a flexible approach, and you'll find that learning AI can be one of the most rewarding adventures. As you continue to explore, engage, and grow within the AI landscape, remember that every piece of knowledge gained is a step toward a future where AI and human ingenuity combine to create incredible possibilities.

By now, you're equipped with the tools to craft a learning path that's uniquely yours, rich with resources tailored to every stage of your journey, and flexible enough to adapt to your evolving interests and goals. As we wrap up this chapter, remember that your AI learning adventure is just that—yours. It's a path that will grow and change as you do, filled with challenges to overcome and milestones to celebrate.

Keep pushing forward, stay curious, and let your passions guide you. Next, we'll dive into the fascinating world of AI applications across various industries, exploring how AI is both a field of study and a dynamic tool that is reshaping our world.

---

1. https://podcast.emerj.com/

2. https://podcasts.apple.com/us/podcast/ai-alignment-with-rohin-shah/id1091344047?i=1000468569858

Chapter 3

Generative AI and Its Creative Potential.

G enerative AI represents a fascinating frontier where algorithms transcend analysis to become creative entities. This chapter explores how AI is expanding the boundaries of creativity, from generating written content to composing music. We'll examine the possibilities and challenges of this exciting development in AI technology and consider its implications for various creative fields.

3.1 Generative AI: An Introduction to Creative Machines

Have you ever felt like unleashing your inner Picasso or Shakespeare but found yourself staring at a blank canvas or blinking cursor? Well, what if I told you there's a kind of AI designed to be your creative sidekick? Yes, enter Generative AI, your soon-to-be partner in the creative process, reshaping fields from art to advertising and beyond. Let's dive into the fascinating world of creative machines!

Generative AI stands out in the AI family for its ability to create something new from scratch. Unlike other AI forms, which analyze data and make predictions (like forecasting the weather or recommending what series to binge next), generative AI is about innovation. It's like having a Roomba that doesn't just vacuum your living room but rearranges your furniture to optimize feng shui and ambiance! At its core, generative AI works by learning from a vast swath of existing data—text, images, music, video—and then uses this learned information to generate new creations that are original yet reminiscent of its training data. This means it can write a fairy tale, compose a serenade, or even whip up a recipe for a cake that might become your new favorite dessert.

One of the stars of the generative AI show is the Generative Adversarial Network or GAN for short. Picture two AIs in a friendly duel: one, the Creator, tries to make something new, and the other, the Critic, judges if it's good enough or just a copycat. The Creator generates new content, and the Critic evaluates it against the real deal. Through this continuous feedback loop, the Creator gets better and better, striving to finally convince the Critic with something indistinguishably authentic. Besides being a technological marvel, this process is also a dance of innovation, pushing the boundaries of what machines can create.

Now, let's tackle a spicy question: Can machines really be creative? Traditionally, creativity has been viewed as a uniquely human trait bound up with consciousness and emotion. But generative AI challenges this notion by producing works that can be startlingly inventive and nuanced to the untrained eye (or even the trained one). From algorithms that paint new Rembrandts to systems that write poetry, generative AI is expanding the scope of machine capability, showing us that creativity might not be solely the province of human minds.

The applications of generative AI are as varied as they are fascinating. In the art world, AI-generated pieces sell for hefty sums, sparking debates about the nature of art and creativity. In recording studios, AI composes tracks that push the boundaries of genre, rhythm, and harmony. In the literary community, AI programs write novels and short stories, experimenting with styles and narratives that offer readers fresh literary experiences.

But there is more. Generative AI also has practical applications that are changing the game in industries like marketing and product design, where it can generate innovative product concepts and advertising copy that resonates with target audiences. The implications here stretch far and wide, not just economically but ethically and philosophically, as we reconsider the role of human creativity in an age where machines can mimic—and sometimes exceed—our own creative outputs.

As we peel back the layers of generative AI, we find ourselves fascinated by its capabilities and questioning some of the very constructs that define human experience. How we navigate this new terrain will undoubtedly be one of the defining challenges of our technological age. Will we view generative AI as a tool, a collaborator, or a competitor? Only time will tell, but one thing is certain—the creative journey with AI is just beginning, promising to be as thrilling as it is unpredictable. So, let's keep our minds open and our curiosity piqued. Who knows? The next great masterpiece might just come from a source we've never imagined.

3.2 Text and Image Generation: How AI Mimics Creativity

If we want to start using this tool to enhance our own creativity, we first need to understand it better. After all, how much help can your sidekick be if you can't tell it what to do? Let's start with text. One of the key players here is LSTM, which stands for Long Short-Term Memory. It's a type of neural network that's really good at understanding sequences—like sentences in a book or notes in a melody. LSTMs are unique because they can remember information for an extended period, which is essential when you're trying to generate a coherent article or a catchy song.

Moving on to imaging. This is where it gets even more (visually) exciting. Remember the friendly duel between the Creator and the Critic in GANs (Generative Adversarial Networks)? Well, they're not just about proving who's got the upper hand. In the realm of images, GANs have been game-changers. They work by having two parts: one that generates images and one that judges them. The generator makes an image, and the discriminator (the judge) decides whether it looks like a real image or not. Through their back-and-forth, the generator learns to produce incredibly realistic images, from breathtaking landscapes that never existed to portraits of famous people that will have you doing a double-take.

Recently, Singer Katy Perry shared a screenshot showing a message from her mom. It said, "Didn't know you went to the Met. What a gorgeous gown! You look like the Rose Parade. You are your own float, lol." Meanwhile, Katy never attended the Met Gala. The picture was AI-generated and so lifelike that it even fooled her own mother!

Can it get even more impressive? It sure can! Enter stage—creative collaboration. Imagine working alongside AI not as a tool but as a creative partner. Artists, writers, and creators of all kinds are beginning to collaborate with AI to push the boundaries of creativity. For instance, an artist might use an AI to generate a series of background landscapes over which they can paint their characters. A writer might use AI to develop different story scenarios, which they can refine and weave into a complex narrative. This synergy can enhance human creativity, opening up new possibilities and perspectives that might not have been explored otherwise.

And then there's the debate of authenticity and originality. Can something created by AI truly be considered original, or does it simply mimic human creativity? This is a hot topic in the art world and beyond, stirring up questions about the nature of creativity itself. Is creativity only valid when it originates from a conscious, emotional being? Or is it about the output itself, regardless of its source? These questions challenge our traditional views on art and authorship, inviting us to rethink what it means to be creative in the first place.

As we explore the capabilities and marvel at the creations of generative AI, we're not just looking at a technological evolution; we're witnessing a fascinating expansion of what it means to create. Whether it's in writing poignant pieces of literature or crafting visual masterpieces, AI is here not just to imitate but to inspire, challenge, and potentially even redefine the essence of creativity. Next time you come across a piece of AI-generated content, take a moment to appreciate the complex interplay of technology and artistry that brought it to life.

3.3 The Role of Generative AI in Music and Art

Have you already experienced a concert enhanced by AI? Or even more extreme, composed and performed in real-time by AI. These are not scenes from a futuristic movie but current trials in the music world. It showcases precisely how generative AI is transforming music production today. AI is no longer just a tool for mixing tracks but has stepped into the spotlight as a composer and performer. Algorithms learn from vast databases of music spanning classical to contemporary pop and then generate new compositions that are both fresh and familiar.

One fascinating aspect of generative AI in music is its role in live performances. Picture a DJ booth manned not by a human but by an AI, responding in real-time to the crowd's reactions. This AI can tweak its beats and melodies on the fly, adapting to the audience's vibe. Beyond adapting to the mood, it's about creating a unique, never-before-heard musical experience for each audience. Even the most talented human DJs might find this level of personalization challenging to achieve consistently.

Beyond live performance, generative AI is also changing how music is composed and produced. Algorithms can now create complex, multi-layered pieces that span genres and styles. Surpassing mimicking existing music, it explores new sonic landscapes. AI can collaborate with musicians and producers, offering new melodies and harmonies they would have never conceived otherwise. This collaboration can be particularly empowering for solo artists, giving them the ability to simulate a full band or orchestra and thus expand their creative possibilities.

Transitioning to the visual arts, the impact of generative AI is equally profound. Conventionally, an artist will sketch out a concept for a landscape painting and choose a particular style to bring this sketch to life. With generative AI, this initial sketch can then be translated into a detailed artwork in various styles—from watercolor to oil painting. The AI can suggest alterations or enhancements, interactively working with the artist to co-create artworks that blend human imagination with algorithmic precision.

In digital art, AI algorithms generate complex patterns and textures used in virtual reality environments, video games, and as digital backdrops for movies. This capability not only speeds up the creative process but also offers artists a new set of tools for expression. They can experiment with AI-generated elements, tweaking and combining them in novel ways to create artworks that are impossible to achieve by human hands alone.

As mentioned earlier, the emergence of generative AI in the arts has sparked a vibrant debate about the nature of creativity and the role of technology in the creative process. For many artists, AI is a liberating force, opening up new pathways for expression and the ability to experiment with techniques and styles that were previously out of reach. For others, there's a fear that AI might overshadow human creativity, pushing artists into a race against machines that can churn out works faster and possibly with more precision.

However, rather than viewing AI as a competitor, it can be more productive to see it as a catalyst transforming the creative landscape. This transformation is all about making art easier to produce and more accessible. With AI, artists who may have physical limitations or lack traditional training can express themselves in ways that were previously unavailable to them. This democratization of art could lead to a more inclusive and diverse cultural landscape enriched by voices that have been underrepresented in the arts.

Moreover, the use of AI in art challenges us to redefine what we consider to be art and creativity. It encourages a broader appreciation of how technology can be an integral part of the creative process rather than just a tool for replication or automation. As we continue to explore this new territory, the interaction between human and artificial creativity is likely to evolve in unexpected ways, leading to new forms of artistic expression that might blur the lines between the creator and the creation.

The vista is thrilling as we peer into the crystal ball to speculate on the future of creativity in an AI-driven world. AI is setting the stage for a new era of creative professions where technology enhances human creativity, making it more interactive, personalized, and accessible. However, the challenge lies in ensuring that this fusion does not stifle human creativity but rather amplifies it, allowing artists to explore new dimensions.

In the grand tapestry of the creative industries, AI's threads are weaving new patterns that might initially seem alien but soon could become the new norm. As these technologies continue to evolve, they promise to redefine existing art forms and give birth to new ones, testing the limits of what we currently perceive as creativity. The key to thriving in this evolving landscape is a blend of curiosity, adaptability, and a relentless pursuit of creative excellence powered by both human and artificial muses.

FUN FACT: did you know all the images in this book have been generated by AI? I wanted to show you the potential and, at the same time, display some of the current limitations. you might find some people have 6 or even 8 fingers or that some words are misspelled or simply don't make sense. while AI image generation isn't quite there yet, I hope you can appreciate how truly mindblowing it is that an Artificial Intelligence can come up with such images based on a few simple prompts.

3.4 Understanding GPT-4 and Other Language Models: Capabilities and Limitations

In the last couple of months, you may have needed some chat support online, and you've encountered a form of AI developed from language models like GPT-3, Claude, or Gemini without even realizing it! These state-of-the-art models are the wizards of the AI world when it comes to understanding and generating human-like text. They aren't just any old chatbots; they're some of the most sophisticated language-processing AI models to date, trained on mind-boggling amounts of data to make their conversation skills top-notch.

GPT-4 (Generative Pre-trained Transformer 4), developed by OpenAI, has been a game-changer in natural language processing. Its capabilities extend beyond mere text generation; it's also about understanding context and nuance in language, which is no small feat. For instance, GPT-4 can continue a story given an initial prompt, maintaining the style and character development with eerie accuracy. It can summarize long articles, create content based on specified keywords, and even answer questions on an almost inexhaustible list of topics.

But GPT-4 isn't the only star in the language model universe. Claude, developed by Anthropic, is another powerful model that has gained attention for its ability to engage in more focused and coherent conversations. One of Claude's standout features is its strong performance in tasks that require a deeper understanding of context and the ability to provide more specific and relevant responses.

Gemini, created by AI21 Labs, is yet another notable language model. It's known for its ability to generate high-quality text that is difficult to distinguish from human-written content. Gemini's strength lies in its adaptability to various writing styles and its ability to produce creative and engaging outputs.

While these language models have impressive capabilities, they also come with their own sets of challenges and limitations. One of the most significant concerns is bias, as these models learn from the vast amounts of data available on the internet, which can include biased or misleading information. This raises questions about the fairness and objectivity of the information they generate. Reliability is another issue, as these models can sometimes generate plausible but inaccurate responses, leading to potential misinformation. And then there are the ethical concerns, such as the potential for misuse in generating fake content or impersonating real people, which can have serious consequences.

As language models like GPT-3, Claude, and Gemini continue to evolve, their integration into various applications will likely become more seamless and widespread. They have the potential to not just change but revolutionize how we interact with technology, making it more natural and intuitive. Imagine a world where you can have a conversation with your computer or smartphone just like you would with a human. However, it's crucial to approach these models with a critical eye, understanding their limitations and the need for human oversight in their development and deployment.

The developmental trajectory for GPT-4 and its successors is focused on tackling these challenges. Enhancements in AI models are aimed at reducing bias and increasing reliability. These developments will involve more sophisticated training techniques, better datasets carefully vetted for quality and diversity, and more advanced algorithms capable of understanding context and subtleties in language with greater precision.

As these models continue to evolve, their integration into everyday applications will become more seamless and widespread, making interactions with AI more natural and productive. Whether it's helping you draft an email, tutoring you on a complex scientific concept, or even entertaining you with a creatively written story, GPT-4 is set to redefine our interaction with technology. It promises a future where AI and humans collaborate more closely, each learning from and enhancing the other's capabilities. So, next time you encounter a particularly articulate chatbot, have fun with it! Take it for a spin and see what it can do.

3.5 The Future of Content Creation with AI

When thinking about creating content, whether writing a blog, designing a graphic, or shooting the next viral video, you've probably considered using several different tools to help you accomplish this goal. What if the same old tools you've been using for years could get a turbo boost from AI? In the world of content creation, AI is quickly becoming a superpower, offering tools and possibilities that are transforming bare-bones ideas into elaborate, polished outputs. And the best part? These tools are becoming more intelligent, intuitive, and aligned with individual creator needs as we interact with them.

Elevating content creation with AI starts with the realization that these technologies are not replacements for human creativity but are supplements that enhance, refine, and expedite the creative process. For instance, AI-driven software can now analyze the emotional impact of a film script, suggest edits for stronger narrative arcs, or even recommend music that enhances the mood of a scene. These tools are like having a personal assistant versed in Oscar-winning filmmaking techniques! Similarly, AI tools can help overcome writer's block by suggesting sentence completions, generating content ideas based on trending topics, or ensuring that the tone of an article matches the intended audience. This kind of support is like having a little birdie constantly tuned into the spirit of the times, whispering the secrets of capturing the audience's attention in your ear.

In addition to making things easier and faster, it's about making them more personalized and customized. AI's ability to analyze vast amounts of data means it can understand preferences and behaviors at an individual level. This capability allows creators to tailor their content to the nuances of their target audience with unprecedented precision. Imagine you're a fashion retailer; AI can help you design a marketing campaign that aligns perfectly with the purchasing habits, style preferences, and even the mood patterns of your customers.

However, as we navigate this exciting terrain, several challenges loom on the horizon, particularly concerning copyright issues and the preservation of the human touch. As AI becomes more adept at creating content that rivals human-made pieces, the lines around copyright ownership blur. Who owns a piece of content that an AI created based on prompts from a human creator? The answer isn't straightforward and is currently paving the way for new legal frameworks. Moreover, while AI can mimic many human creative abilities, there's a depth of emotion, a nuance of feeling, or a burst of spontaneity that's inherently human. Preserving this human touch—this soul—in AI-generated content is crucial. It ensures that the technology remains a tool of expression rather than becoming a sterile, albeit efficient, content generator.

The vision for content creation with AI is one of vibrance and collaboration. We're moving towards a future where AI becomes a creative partner, working alongside humans in a symbiotic relationship. This partnership promises to unlock new creative potentials by combining the best of both worlds: the speed, efficiency, and data-processing capabilities of AI with the emotional depth, intuition, and personal experience of human creators. Imagine a filmmaker working with AI to dynamically alter a film's plot based on real-time audience reactions in test screenings or a novelist using AI to explore different story arcs before deciding on the one that best expresses their vision.

This collaborative process could redefine storytelling, art, and design, making them more interactive and adaptive. As AI technologies evolve, they could allow creators to experiment with complex, multi-layered projects that would be too resource-intensive or technically challenging without AI—leading to richer, more immersive experiences that are simultaneously deeply personal and widely accessible.

As we stand on the brink of these developments, it's clear that AI is not just altering the landscape of content creation but is also inviting us to rethink the boundaries of creativity. The tools are here, and they're getting smarter by the day. How we choose to use them will shape the content we produce, the stories we tell, and the experiences we share. The future of content creation with AI is not just about maintaining pace with technology but about moving forward together, creating with more intention, inclusivity, and interaction.

3.6 Ethical Considerations in Generative AI

Navigating the waters of generative AI isn't just about unleashing a whirlwind of creativity; it's also about steering carefully to avoid ethical pitfalls that could ripple across societies and generations. Think of it as being handed the keys to a flashy, supercharged sports car. It's thrilling, for sure, but without a good set of brakes and some ground rules, things could go sideways quickly. So, let's talk about those brakes and regulations in the world of generative AI, particularly focusing on the ethical challenges, promoting responsible use, and the delicate dance between innovation and ethics.

The ethical challenges in generative AI are both complex and critical. Starting with one of the biggest concerns: the potential for misuse. Just as a hammer can be used to build a house or break a window, generative AI can be extremely harmful if used with ill intent. From deepfakes (synthetic media in which a person in an existing image or video is replaced with someone else's likeness using AI) that could undermine public trust to AI-generated propaganda that can sway public opinion, the misuse of these technologies can have serious consequences. Then there's the question of intellectual property rights. If an AI creates a piece of music or a novel, who owns it? The person who designed the AI? The user who provided the inputs? Or does the AI itself hold some form of digital authorship? These aren't just theoretical questions—they're real issues that creators and legal experts grapple with as AI becomes a more common co-creator in the arts.

Thus, promoting the responsible use of generative AI is crucial to ensure this technology brings more good than harm. This starts with transparency—being clear about when and how AI is used in the creative process. Think about a music album produced with the help of AI. Shouldn't fans know what parts were human and what parts were machine? In the same way that clothing labels specify the materials used in a garment, information about AI involvement could help audiences understand precisely what they're appreciating. Another part of responsible use is setting standards for AI behavior—yes, AI behavior. Setting these standards is done by programming ethical guidelines into the AI's operational code, similar to instilling good values in a child. It's about embedding ethical considerations into every layer of the AI development process, from the drawing board to the final output.

Balancing innovation with ethics in generative AI is akin to walking a tightrope. Lean too much on either side, and you risk falling off. On one side, you've got the boundless potential of AI to transform creative industries, offering tools that could help artists and creators do things they've only dreamed of. On the other, there are valid concerns about the implications of these technologies—ethical, social, and legal. Striking a balance requires a collaborative approach involving not just technologists but also ethicists, industry stakeholders, and policymakers. It's about creating a resilient foundation that supports innovation while simultaneously protecting society from potential negative impacts.

Now, let's talk about the role of policy and regulation. Just as traffic laws help keep roads safe, well-thought-out policies and regulations are essential for guiding the use of generative AI. Putting such policies in place doesn't mean stifling creativity with red tape. Instead, it's about ensuring that these powerful tools are used in ways that benefit society and foster a healthy, ethical, creative environment. For instance, regulations could require companies to disclose the use of AI in their products, similar to how tech companies must inform users about their data collection practices in their privacy policies. Policies could also incentivize the development of ethical AI systems through tax breaks or grants, encouraging innovators to prioritize ethical considerations as much as technical advancements.

As we wrap up this exploration of the ethical landscape of generative AI, remember that it's about much more than just avoiding pitfalls. It's about paving a way forward that respects creative integrity, protects individual rights, and promotes a culture of responsible innovation. By addressing these ethical considerations head-on, we can ensure that generative AI serves as a force for good, enhancing human creativity and enriching our cultural heritage rather than undermining it. As we turn the page to the next chapter, let's carry forward this mindset of thoughtful, ethical engagement with technology, ready to explore new horizons with both enthusiasm and caution.

Chapter 4

AI in Everyday Life

E ver felt like the web knows you a little too well? You're just thinking about getting those concert tickets, and bam, an ad pops up with a discount on them. This is AI at work in your daily online experience, tailoring everything from the ads you see to the posts in your feed based on your past behavior. Let's pull back the curtain and see how this digital wizardry happens.

4.1 How AI Personalizes Your Online Experience

The magic starts with data—oodles and oodles of it. Every click you make, every item you browse, and every term you search is picked up by AI algorithms. This data is like gold for AI systems, which analyze patterns in your online behavior to customize your digital experiences. It's similar to a chef who knows you despise olives and love extra cheese, so they tailor your dish each time you visit. AI uses algorithms to predict what content will keep you scrolling, which products you might buy, or which songs you want to add to your playlist.

These algorithms are often part of larger systems known as recommendation engines. They work quietly behind the scenes on platforms like Netflix, Amazon, and Spotify, crafting personalized experiences that feel almost intuitive. Take Netflix, for instance. Have you ever noticed how it knows the type of show you're in the mood for? That's because its AI has been learning from your viewing history, the ratings you've given various shows, and even what you've stopped watching midway.

The benefits of AI-driven personalization are substantial. First off, it enhances your user experience. These platforms make your online time more efficient and enjoyable by filtering out the noise and honing in on what interests you. No more slogging through pages of irrelevant content or feeling overwhelmed by too many choices—AI makes your digital spaces feel designed just for you.

Finding a band you love on a Spotify playlist you didn't create or binge-watching a series on Netflix you hadn't even heard of before it popped up on your recommended list are just examples of how AI can introduce you to potential new favorites. AI can nudge you toward the right content by analyzing trends and correlating your tastes with other users who like what you like.

While it's great to feel like the internet gets you, this personalization has pitfalls, especially concerning privacy. With AI constantly analyzing your online behavior and watching every move you make, it is understandable to become a bit uneasy, wondering who else might access this data and how it could be used.

Protecting your information starts with understanding what data you're sharing and adjusting your settings accordingly. Most platforms offer privacy settings, allowing you to control the data you share. Think of it as setting boundaries in a relationship. You decide what you're comfortable sharing and what remains off-limits.

The future of AI in personalization is likely to get even more sophisticated. An AI that doesn't just react to your behavior but anticipates your needs before you even articulate them. We're talking about AI that could help manage your calendar, suggesting the perfect timing for your next vacation based on your work schedule and travel preferences, or AI that knows to order groceries when you're running low, even adding your favorite snack just as a new season of your favorite series drops.

As these technologies evolve, the key will be finding a balance between highly personalized experiences and maintaining user privacy and trust. It's a dynamic dance between offering convenience and safeguarding our digital footprints. Staying informed and proactive about our digital choices will be paramount as we navigate this landscape. After all, while it's fantastic to have a digital experience tailored just for you, keeping the reins on what we share is equally important.

As AI continues to weave its way deeper into the fabric of our daily digital inter-actions, staying aware and engaged with how we interact with this technology will shape our online experiences and the broader digital culture. So next time you marvel at how well your streaming service knows your taste in TV shows, give a nod to the AI working hard behind the scenes—and maybe check your privacy settings just to keep that relationship healthy.

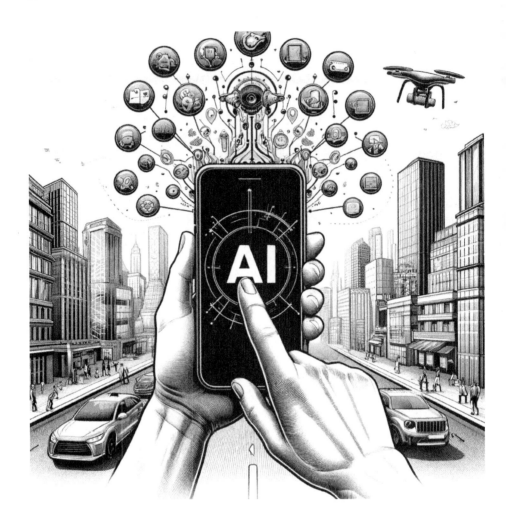

4.2 Smart Homes and AI: Enhancing Daily Living

How good does it feel to walk into your living room on a scorching day and find it waiting for you, perfectly chilled? Or have the lights turned on just how you like them as you enter the door? That's the magic of smart home technologies at work. These are more than fancy gadgets to show off when your friends come over; they're practical, everyday technologies that make life easier and more comfortable. AI-powered smart homes are like having a roommate who always remembers your preferences, only this roommate never leaves their smelly socks lying around or finishes the milk—again.

Smart home technologies encompass many devices that automate tasks and improve energy efficiency. Smart thermostats, for example, learn your schedule and temperature preferences to optimize heating and cooling, ensuring your home is always at the perfect temperature while also saving energy. Then, there are smart lights that adjust brightness and color based on the time of day or even your mood, creating the perfect ambiance without you having to flick a switch. And let's not forget smart security systems that keep an eye on your home, alerting you to any unusual activity and providing peace of mind, whether tucked in bed or halfway around the world.

These technologies are part of the Internet of Things (IoT)*, a network of devices that communicate and operate together to make your home smarter. They gather data through sensors or user inputs, which AI algorithms analyze to make real-time decisions. For instance, a smart thermostat might notice that you usually turn down the heat at night and start lowering the temperature automatically as bedtime approaches. Or a smart security system might recognize your family's faces and only alert you if someone unfamiliar is spotted.

The convenience of smart home technologies is undeniable. Imagine waking up to the smell of coffee brewing or having your bath drawn at the perfect temperature when you come home after a long day. These small luxuries can significantly enhance your daily living, making routine tasks a breeze and allowing you more time to relax and enjoy life. But it's not just about comfort; it's also about efficiency. Smart homes can lead to substantial energy savings, which is good for your wallet and the planet.

However, as with all technologies, smart homes also have their share of security implications. The more connected your home is, the more potential entry points there are for hackers. A compromised security system could lead to privacy breaches or even physical threats. It cannot be mentioned enough how critical it is to secure these smart devices. Regularly updating software, using strong, unique passwords, and employing encryption can help mitigate these risks. It's also wise to consider a security system that operates independently of your other smart home devices, ensuring that your home's security remains intact even if one device is compromised.

Despite their benefits, adopting smart home technologies can be challenging. High costs and perceived complexity can deter many potential users. Moreover, there's a significant accessibility gap; those who could benefit the most from these technologies, such as people advanced in age or dealing with disabilities, often face the highest barriers to adoption. Developing user-friendly devices that are also affordable is of vital importance to ensure accessibility to all. Educational initiatives that demystify smart home technology can also play a key role in making these innovations more approachable to a broader audience.

4.3 AI in Healthcare: From Diagnosis to Treatment

When visiting the doctor's office, there may have been a time when you felt like just another name on an appointment list. The bold vision is that AI will change that in the near future, making healthcare less about the waiting room and more about you. Picture this: AI not only helping doctors diagnose diseases faster and more accurately but also tailoring treatment plans just for you. Instead of having to repeat yourself over and over again, there will be a digital assistant who's read every file, seen every case, and remembers every detail of your last visits, all tuned to help optimize your health.

Diving into diagnostics, AI is like the Sherlock Holmes of healthcare, especially when reading medical images. Whether spotting a tiny tumor on an MRI or detecting early signs of diabetic retinopathy in eye scans, AI is making waves. It works through sophisticated algorithms that can analyze images, recognize patterns, and even catch details the human eye might miss. For instance, AI systems trained on thousands of X-rays can learn to detect anomalies such as fractures or lung nodules with impressive accuracy. The aim here isn't to replace the radiologists; it's about giving them superpowers to see more, know more, and diagnose faster with AI as their helper.

The beauty of AI in diagnostics doesn't stop at imagery. It extends to predictive diagnostics, where AI algorithms sift through heaps of data—everything from genetic information to lifestyle habits—to predict health risks before they become issues. For example, knowing your risk of heart disease just from an app that tracks your diet, exercise, and family history, all crunched and analyzed by AI. This proactive approach isn't just futuristic; it's happening now, transforming check-ups from routine to revolutionary.

Moving on from diagnosis to treatment, AI's role becomes even more personal: a customized healthcare strategy crafted just for you. AI in treatment planning means algorithms can help doctors determine the most effective approaches based on big data—including vast amounts of research and prior patient outcomes. Again, not to replace doctors but to empower them with a tool that offers a helicopter view of all possible treatments, predicting which will work best for you.

In patient care, AI becomes a 24/7 monitoring system, keeping an eye on patient vitals and alerting healthcare staff at the first sign of trouble. For patients managing chronic conditions like diabetes or hypertension, AI-enhanced devices can track everything from blood sugar levels to blood pressure, providing real-time feedback and recommendations. It's like having a nurse in your pocket reminding you to take your medication or suggesting a walk after a fatty meal.

Personalized medicine is another frontier where AI is making a mark. By analyzing your genetic makeup, AI can predict how you'll respond to certain medications, allowing for specifically effective treatments for you, minimizing side effects, and maximizing efficacy. This tailored treatment approach ensures that healthcare is not one-size-fits-all but custom-fitted, just like a perfectly tailored tuxedo.

Ethical considerations abound when using AI in healthcare, particularly concerning patient privacy and the reliability of AI diagnoses. Handling sensitive health data with AI involves ensuring this information is secure and used appropriately. It's crucial to have robust data protection measures similar to how banks use sophisticated security systems to protect their client's financial information because personal health data is just as valuable.

The reliability of AI in making diagnoses or treatment recommendations also raises ethical questions. While AI can process data at superhuman speeds, it's still prone to errors, especially if trained on flawed data. Ensuring AI's accuracy and handling its recommendations with a critical eye is needed to prevent misdiagnoses or inappropriate treatments. It's about integrating AI tools to complement, not complicate, the healthcare process.

Moving forward, one major hurdle to overcome is the integration of AI into existing healthcare systems. It's not just about the technology itself but about adapting workflows, training staff, and updating policies to accommodate AI's role in healthcare. There's also the challenge of public trust. Getting people to trust AI with their health is arduous, given the intimate nature of medical care and the potential risks involved.

However, the future prospects of AI in healthcare are awe-inspiring. We're looking at a world where AI could help eradicate diseases through early detection and personalized prevention plans. A world where AI-driven robots assist in surgeries, making procedures less invasive and recovery times faster. The possibilities are vast, and the potential immense. As we navigate these prospects, we must focus on harnessing AI's capabilities responsibly, ensuring that this powerful tool makes healthcare better, not just more high-tech. As we continue to explore the expanding capabilities of AI in healthcare, striking a balance between innovation and ethical responsibility must stay at the forefront. After all, at the heart of healthcare is care itself, and preserving this human element amidst technological advancement will truly define AI's success in this vital field.

4.4 The Role of AI in Financial Services

Maybe you are from an older generation like me and can still remember when you walked into a bank and the teller knew you by name. Now, imagine that the teller isn't a person but an AI system. On top of knowing your name, it also knows your financial goals, habits, and even your concerns about your retirement plan. Equipped with deep knowledge about your finances, the AI is ready to offer customized banking advice in mere seconds. Welcome to the new banking era powered by AI, where everything from customer service to fraud detection is getting a tech-savvy overhaul.

In the realm of banking, AI is like the multi-tool Swiss Army knife that keeps on giving. It's reshaping how banks operate, making them more efficient, customer-friendly, and secure. For starters, consider fraud detection. AI systems are trained to sniff out patterns that might indicate fraudulent activity. These systems analyze thousands of transactions in real-time, looking for anomalies that could suggest something fishy. For example, if an account suddenly makes several high-value transactions in a short period, the AI might flag it for review. This kind of surveillance helps protect not just the banks' money but yours.

Customer service is another area where AI is making significant inroads. Chatbots, those friendly little chat windows that pop up when navigating a bank's website, are AI's frontline soldiers. They can handle a range of queries, from checking account balances to assisting with money transfers, and they're learning all the time. The more interactions they handle, the better they get at solving problems and anticipating customer needs. Need to block a lost credit card at 2 AM? No problem. The chatbot has you covered; no human needed.

Then there's personalized financial advice, a territory traditionally dominated by human financial advisors. Now, AI can fulfill this role by providing customized advice based on a deep analysis of your spending habits, investment history, and financial goals. It constantly analyzes market trends and your financial data to offer tailored advice. This opens up financial planning, making it accessible to more people at a fraction of the cost of a human advisor.

AI's impact is just as transformative, looking at trading and investments. Algorithmic trading, where complex algorithms manage buy and sell orders, is now a staple on Wall Street. These algorithms can process a vast amount of market data, make decisions in fractions of a second, and execute trades faster than any human ever could. This capability not only enhances the efficiency of markets but also can increase the profitability of trading strategies.

Predictive analytics, another AI forte, alters investment strategies by forecasting market trends and asset price movements. By analyzing historical data and identifying patterns, AI can make educated guesses about future market behaviors. This tool is invaluable for investors looking to optimize their investment strategies, providing a data-driven way to assess potential risks and rewards.

However, the use of AI must be governed by strict ethical standards to prevent biases in financial advice or lending practices. For instance, if an AI system denies a loan application, the criteria used should be transparent and fair. There's also the risk of systemic errors—like those that could occur if an algorithmic trading system goes rogue, potentially leading to market instability.

The potential impact on employment in the sector is also significant. While AI might streamline many operations, potentially reducing the need for human staff in routine tasks, it could also create new roles focused on managing and improving AI systems.

As we navigate this dynamic landscape, the financial services industry must not let the drive for innovation negatively impact ethical practices and public trust. As these technologies become more embedded in our financial dealings, staying informed and engaged with how AI is used in this field will benefit everyone, from industry professionals to everyday consumers.

4.5 AI in Education: Personalized Learning Paths

In China, classrooms are already equipped with AI that knows precisely how fast students learn, the topics they find challenging, and the teaching style that pays the most dividends. It is safe to expect this to be rolled out into classrooms closer to home in the near future. In these early stages, the main objective of this technology isn't to replace teachers but rather to allow them to tailor learning experiences uniquely for each student. The focus of AI in the classroom goes beyond the personalization of lesson plans; it also aims to make education more inclusive and engaging.

Personalized learning via AI adjusts to the student's learning speed, scales up the difficulty when cruising through lessons, and takes a different approach if they're struggling. For example, if you're a visual learner, AI can adapt your curriculum to include more videos and interactive graphics instead of text-heavy content. Or, if you're mastering algebra faster than your peers, it might offer you advanced problems to solve, keeping you challenged and engaged. This customization is done through sophisticated algorithms that analyze how you interact with educational content. They notice when you breeze through a quiz or re-watch a particular section of a lecture, and they adjust your learning path accordingly. This tailored approach makes learning more successful, ensuring every student feels included and supported.

AI in educational settings can also predict potential learning outcomes based on your performance trends. This means it can foresee possible future difficulties you might encounter and preemptively adjust the curriculum to address these challenges. Think of it as a GPS navigation system for your education, constantly recalculating the best route to reach your learning destination efficiently.

Moving on to AI tutors and assistants, these are not your typical classroom helpers. They're available 24/7, always ready to help you solve a tricky math problem or explain a complex scientific concept at 4 AM before your big test. These AI systems use natural language processing to understand your questions and provide clear, concise, and correct answers. For instance, if you're stuck on a calculus problem, an AI tutor can guide you through the solution step-by-step, adjusting its explanations based on how well you grasp the concept.

However, as helpful as they are, AI tutors have their limitations. They're fantastic for subjects with clear right or wrong answers, like math or chemistry, but less so for more subjective areas, like literature or art criticism. Here, human teachers' nuanced understanding and emotional depth in discussions about themes or styles are still irreplaceable. So, while AI can help you understand how Hemingway uses dialogue, it might not be the best at exploring the emotional undercurrents of his narratives.

One of the most heartening aspects of AI in education is its ability to make learning more accessible. For students with disabilities, AI-powered tools can be life-changing. Visual impairments, for instance, can transform textbooks into audio formats. At the same time, AI-driven applications can turn spoken language into text for hearing-impaired people. For students in remote or underserved regions, AI education tools can bridge the gap by providing high-quality educational materials and virtual assistance that would otherwise be unavailable. Adopting these tools across the globe means that one's geographical location or physical abilities no longer limit one's learning potential.

The potential for AI in education sparkles with possibilities. We expect to see curriculums entirely crafted around each student's needs and capabilities and entirely new teaching methods designed with the help of AI. However, providing equitable access globally might prove difficult. We need to continue to work towards ensuring these advanced AI tools don't become luxury goods available only to the affluent or those in developed nations. The goal is to use AI not to widen the educational divide but to close it.

As AI continues to evolve, so too will its role in education. Keeping a pulse on these changes will be important to ensure they're steered towards inclusivity and effectiveness. As we venture further into this AI-enhanced educational landscape, the promise of what we might achieve gives us every reason to pay attention—and perhaps even dream a little about all the possibilities that lie ahead.

4.6 Ethical AI Use in Surveillance and Security

Do you remember the movie Minority Report? In this 2002 movie starring Tom Cruise, a specialized police department uses precognitive technology to prevent crimes before they occur. The film prominently features AI-driven facial recognition systems deployed in public spaces, enabling police to identify and apprehend potential criminals. When this movie was released, no one even considered the possibility of this being reality one day. Yet, here we are. AI-powered surveillance technologies are becoming a staple in public safety measures. These systems, equipped with facial recognition and anomaly detection capabilities, are reshaping how we think about security and privacy. Even though these advancements bolster our safety, they stir up significant debates about the ethical implications of mass surveillance and the balance between security and individual privacy in a technologically advanced society.

Surveillance technologies powered by AI are not just about tracking; they're about enhancing the efficiency and effectiveness of security measures. Facial recognition technology, for example, can quickly identify individuals in crowded places, helping law enforcement respond swiftly to potential threats. Then there's anomaly detection, which uses AI to monitor real-time video feeds, pinpointing behaviors or events that deviate from the norm. This could be anything from detecting an unattended bag at an airport to identifying a person in distress. These technologies are invaluable in preempting incidents and ensuring public safety. However, the balance between enhancing safety and protecting individual privacy is delicate. On one hand, we all want to live in a safe environment where threats are quickly identified and dealt with. On the other, no one likes the idea of being watched constantly. This is where the ethical use of surveillance AI comes into play. It's crucial to ensure that these technologies are used in ways that respect individual privacy and civil liberties. For instance, while facial recognition can be a powerful tool for security, it should be deployed judiciously, ensuring it doesn't lead to unwarranted privacy intrusions or become a tool for mass surveillance.

Moreover, the regulatory frameworks governing the use of AI in surveillance are key to maintaining this balance. These frameworks must be robust and clear, outlining how AI surveillance technologies can be used and which safeguards must be in place to protect citizens' rights. Existing regulations like the European GDPR provide a foundation, emphasizing transparency, consent, and the right to privacy. However, as AI technologies evolve, so too must our legal frameworks. They must be adaptable and forward-thinking, anticipating future developments and ensuring that advancements in surveillance technologies are matched by equally robust privacy protections.

For AI deployments to be successful, they must not only be effective but also trusted by the public they serve. This means involving communities in conversations about how AI technologies are used in public safety and ensuring there is a clear and accountable process for addressing any concerns.

As we navigate the complexities of AI in surveillance and security, we must continually assess the trade-offs between safety and privacy. The goal is not just to implement powerful technologies but to do so in a way that respects the ethical considerations at play. By fostering a dialogue between technology developers, policymakers, and the public and by ensuring robust regulatory frameworks are in place, we can harness the benefits of AI-powered surveillance while safeguarding individual rights.

In conclusion, as we wrap up this exploration into AI's role in everyday life, from personalizing your online experiences to enhancing public safety, the overarching theme has been about balance— convenience with privacy, innovation with ethics, and individual needs with societal benefits. In the next chapter, we'll delve into the transformative impact of AI in industries beyond our daily personal interactions, exploring how AI is reshaping sectors like manufacturing, logistics, and more, promising to overhaul the way we produce, deliver, and manage goods and services in an increasingly interconnected world.

Chapter 5

AI Tools and Resources for Beginners

T he vast landscape of AI can be overwhelming for newb. This chapter serves as a comprehensive guide to user-friendly AI tools and resources. We'll navigate through the most accessible platforms for beginners, highlight valuable learning materials, and provide strategies for understanding AI algorithms without advanced technical knowledge. By the chapter's end, you'll be equipped with a practical toolkit to begin your AI journey.

5.1 Top AI Tools Every Beginner Should Know

AI tools have become increasingly accessible to beginners, offering numerous capabilities and applications. These tools can help you get started with AI projects, experiment with different techniques, and gain hands-on experience. Here are some of the top AI tools every beginner should know:

1. TensorFlow[1]: TensorFlow is an open-source software library developed by Google for machine learning and deep learning. It provides a comprehensive ecosystem of tools, libraries, and resources, making it a popular choice for building and deploying ML models. TensorFlow offers a high-level API called Keras, which simplifies the process of creating neural networks.

2. PyTorch[2]: PyTorch is an open-source machine learning library primarily developed by Facebook's AI Research lab. It is known for its dynamic computational graph and ease of use, making it a favorite among researchers and developers. PyTorch provides a flexible and intuitive interface for building and training deep learning models.

3. Scikit-learn[3]: Scikit-learn is a free software machine learning library for the Python programming language. It offers supervised and unsupervised learning algorithms, such as decision trees, random forests, and support vector machines. Scikit-learn is built on top of NumPy, SciPy, and matplotlib, making it easy to integrate with other Python libraries.

4. Keras[4]: Keras is an open-source neural network library written in Python that can run on top of TensorFlow, Microsoft Cognitive Toolkit, R, Theano, or PlaidML. It is designed to enable fast experimentation with deep neural networks and focuses on being user-friendly, modular, and extensible. Keras provides a high-level API for building and training deep learning models.

5. OpenCV[5]: OpenCV (Open Source Computer Vision Library) is an open-source library for computer vision and machine learning. It provides tools and algorithms for tasks such as image and video processing, object detection, and facial recognition. OpenCV is widely used in both academia and industry for computer vision applications.

6. NLTK[6]: NLTK (Natural Language Toolkit) is a suite of libraries and programs for symbolic and statistical natural language processing in Python. It provides tokenization, stemming, tagging, parsing, and semantic reasoning tools. NLTK is often used for teaching and research in natural language processing.

7. SpaCy[7]: SpaCy is an open-source software library for advanced natural language processing in Python. It offers fast and efficient tools for tokenization, named entity recognition, part-of-speech tagging, and dependency parsing. SpaCy is designed to be easy to use and integrates well with other Python libraries.

8. Hugging Face Transformers[8]: Hugging Face Transformers is an open-source library that provides state-of-the-art pre-trained models for natural language processing tasks. It offers a wide range of transformer-based models, such as BERT, GPT, and RoBERTa, which can be fine-tuned for tasks like text classification, question answering, and language translation.

These tools offer a solid foundation for beginners to explore various aspects of AI, from machine learning and deep learning to computer vision and natural language processing. By familiarizing yourself with these tools and their capabilities, you can build your own AI projects and gain practical experience in the field.

5.2 Leveraging AI Resources for Self-Learning

In addition to the AI tools mentioned in the previous section, plenty of free online resources are available that can help beginners learn about AI concepts, techniques, and applications. These resources include online courses, tutorials, books, and communities offering valuable knowledge and self-learning support.

Here are some AI resources you might find useful:

1. **Online Courses:**

   a. Coursera's Machine Learning Course by Andrew Ng[9]: This course provides a comprehensive introduction to machine learning, covering topics such as linear regression, logistic regression, neural networks, and recommender systems.

   b. Google's Machine Learning Crash Course[10]: This course offers a fast-paced introduction to machine learning concepts and techniques, with hands-on exercises using TensorFlow.

   c. edX's Introduction to Artificial Intelligence (AI) Course by Microsoft[11]: This course uses Python and Azure Notebooks to cover the basics of AI, including machine learning, natural language processing, and computer vision.

2. **Tutorials and Blog Posts:**

   a. Machine Learning Mastery[12]: This website offers many tutorials and guides on machine learning, deep learning, and AI, focusing on practical examples and code implementations.

   b. Towards Data Science[13]: This publication on Medium features articles and tutorials on various AI topics written by experts and practitioners in the field.

   c. Analytics Vidhya[14]: This platform provides tutorials, articles, and competitions related to AI, machine learning, and data science.

3. **Books:**

   a. "Python Machine Learning"[15] by Sebastian Raschka and Vahid Mirjalili: This book offers a comprehensive introduction to machine learning using Python, covering data preprocessing, feature selection, and various ML algorithms.

b. "Hands-On Machine Learning with Scikit-Learn, Keras, and Tensor-Flow"[16] by Aurélien Géron: This book provides a practical approach to machine learning and deep learning, with code examples using popular libraries and frameworks.

c. "Python Crash Course"[17] by Eric Matthes: This hands-on guide to Python focuses on the practical skills and understanding you need to write programs and develop functional applications.

4. **Communities and Forums:**

a. Kaggle[18]: Kaggle is a platform for data science and machine learning competitions, offering a large community of practitioners and a wide range of datasets and tutorials.

b. Stack Overflow[19]: Stack Overflow is a popular Q&A platform for programmers, with a dedicated section for AI and machine learning topics.

c. Reddit's Machine Learning Subreddit[20]This subreddit is a community of AI enthusiasts, researchers, and practitioners that offers discussions, news, and resources related to machine learning and AI.

d. LinkedIn's AI and Machine Learning groups[21]

These resources, some free, some paid, can help you create a structured learning path tailored to your interests and goals. Combining theoretical knowledge with practical exercises and projects reinforces understanding and gaining hands-on experience.

When using these resources, pace yourself and avoid information overload. Start with foundational concepts and gradually progress to more advanced topics. Engage with the communities and forums to ask questions, seek guidance, and learn from others' experiences.

Remember that self-learning requires discipline and persistence. Set realistic goals, create a study schedule, and consistently dedicate time to your AI learning journey. As you progress, apply your knowledge to real-world projects and contribute to the AI community by sharing your insights and experiences.

5.3 Understanding AI Algorithms Without Coding

Coding is essential for developing AI applications; luckily, gaining a conceptual understanding of AI algorithms without delving into the intricacies of programming is possible. Understanding the principles behind these algorithms can help you grasp how AI systems work and make informed decisions when applying AI techniques to real-world problems.

One effective way to understand AI algorithms without coding is through interactive visualizations and simulations. These tools allow users to explore the behavior of algorithms by adjusting parameters, observing outputs, and gaining insights into how different components interact. Some popular resources for interactive AI algorithm visualizations include:

1. TensorFlow Playground[22]: This web-based tool lets users experiment with neural networks, visualize their learning, and make predictions based on different configurations and hyperparameters.

2. Distill[23]: A platform that provides interactive articles and visualizations explaining complex AI concepts, such as feature visualization, activation atlases, and dimensionality reduction.

3. GAN Lab[24]: GAN Lab is an interactive visualization tool that demonstrates the working principles of Generative Adversarial Networks (GANs) and allows users to experiment with different architectures and training strategies.

Let's dive deeper into understanding AI algorithms using high-level explanations and analogies.

K-means clustering is an unsupervised learning algorithm for finding patterns in data without any pre-existing labels or output categories provided. It aims to partition n observations into k clusters, where each observation belongs to the cluster with the nearest mean. The "n observations" refers to the total number of data points or instances in your dataset. For example, if you have a dataset of customer information, each customer record would be considered one "observation." The "k clusters" refer to a specified number of groups into which the algorithm will cluster or divide the n observations based on their similarity.

In k-means clustering:

- You have a dataset with n rows/observations

- You choose a value for k, which is the number of clusters you want to group the observations into

- The algorithm assigns each observation to one of the k clusters based on its feature values and proximity to the cluster centroids

- It tries to minimize the variance within clusters while maximizing the variance between clusters

Some examples:

- If you have 10,000 customer records (n=10,000 observations) and you set k=5, k-means will divide those 10,000 customers into 5 clusters based on similarities in their data.

- If you have 50,000 image files (n=50,000) and set k=20, it will group those 50,000 images into 20 distinct clusters.

The user predetermines the value of k before running k-means based on the problem context. In summary, n is just the number of data instances, while k is the number of clusters you want to group those n instances into.

Decision trees are a supervised learning algorithm that creates a tree-like model of decisions and their possible consequences. Imagine you want to decide whether to go for a picnic based on the weather conditions. You start by asking the most important question at the tree's root: "Is it raining?" If the answer is "yes," you decide not to go for the picnic. If the answer is "no," you move to the following question: "Is it windy?" If it's windy, you might consider other factors like temperature or humidity before deciding. If it's not windy, you decide to go for the picnic. This process of asking questions and making decisions based on the answers forms a decision tree.

Reinforcement learning is a type of machine learning where an agent learns to make decisions by interacting with an environment. Imagine training a pet dog to perform tricks. You start by letting the dog explore its environment and perform random actions. Whenever the dog performs the desired action, like sitting down when you say "sit," you reward it with a treat. If the dog performs an undesired action, you withhold the treat. Over time, the dog learns to associate specific actions with positive rewards and performs those actions more frequently. This is how reinforcement learning works – the AI agent learns to make decisions based on the rewards it receives from the environment.

Some of these rewards could include:

- Positive reinforcement - Verbal praise, an encouraging feedback signal, or any indicator that the agent's action was correct or desired.

- Access to more data/environments - Allowing the agent to explore new training data or environments as a reward for performing well.

- Computational resources - Increasing the agent's available computing power, memory, or other resources as a reward.

Case studies are another effective way to understand AI algorithms in action. Let's look at a few examples:

1. Netflix uses collaborative filtering algorithms to recommend movies and TV shows based on a user's viewing history and similar users' preferences. By analyzing the watching patterns of millions of users, Netflix can suggest content that a particular user is likely to enjoy, keeping them engaged with the platform.

2. Google Maps uses graph algorithms, such as Dijkstra's algorithm, to find the shortest path between two points on a map. By considering factors like distance, traffic, and road closures, Google Maps can provide optimized routing options to help users navigate efficiently.

3. Facebook uses deep learning algorithms, particularly convolutional neural networks (CNNs), for automatic face recognition and tagging in photos. By training on millions of labeled facial images, Facebook's AI can accurately identify and tag individuals in new photos uploaded to the platform.

These case studies demonstrate how AI algorithms are applied in real-world scenarios to solve complex problems and provide valuable services to users. By combining high-level explanations, analogies, and real-world examples, you can gain a solid understanding of AI algorithms without delving into the intricacies of coding. This conceptual understanding will help you appreciate the capabilities and limitations of AI systems and make informed decisions when working with AI tools and platforms.

5.4 Using AI Responsibly: A Guide to Ethical AI Tools

As AI tools become more powerful and accessible, it's essential to understand the importance of using them responsibly and ethically. AI systems can significantly impact individuals, society, and the environment, and it's essential to consider the potential consequences of deploying these technologies.

When exploring AI tools, prioritize those that align with ethical principles and promote responsible AI development. Some key ethical considerations include:

1. Data Privacy and Security: AI tools often rely on large amounts of data, including personal and sensitive information. It's critical to ensure that this data is collected, stored, and used in a secure and privacy-preserving manner. When choosing AI tools, look for those that have robust data protection measures in place, such as encryption and secure authentication mechanisms. Be aware of the data privacy policies of the tools you use and ensure that they comply with relevant regulations, such as the General Data Protection Regulation (GDPR) or the California Consumer Privacy Act (CCPA).

2. Bias and Fairness: AI tools can inadvertently perpetuate or amplify biases present in the data they are trained on or the algorithms they use. Bias in the data can lead to unfair or discriminatory outcomes, particularly for marginalized or underrepresented groups. For instance, an AI system used for predictive policing that is trained on historical crime data may disproportionately flag specific neighborhoods or demographics as higher risk, leading to over-policing and perpetuating systemic biases in law enforcement practices. When selecting AI tools, consider those developed with fairness and non-discrimination in mind. Seek out tools that have undergone rigorous testing for bias and have mechanisms in place to mitigate any identified biases. Be aware of the potential limitations and biases of the tools you use and consider their outputs' social and ethical implications.

3. Transparency and Accountability: The decision-making processes of AI tools can often be opaque, making it difficult to understand how they arrive at specific outputs or recommendations. This lack of transparency can be problematic, particularly in high-stakes domains such as healthcare, criminal justice, or financial services. When choosing AI tools, prioritize those that clearly explain their inner workings and decision-making processes. Look for tools that offer interpretability features or have undergone third-party audits for transparency. Hold developers accountable for the outcomes of their AI tools and ensure that there are mechanisms in place for redress in case of adverse consequences.

4. Human Oversight and Control: While AI tools can automate many tasks and provide valuable insights, maintaining human oversight and control is paramount, particularly in critical decision-making processes. AI tools should be designed to augment and support human decision-making rather

than replace it entirely. When using AI tools, ensure that appropriate human-in-the-loop mechanisms are in place, allowing for human intervention and final decision-making authority. Be aware of the limitations of AI tools and use them in conjunction with human expertise and judgment.

To help you navigate the landscape of ethical AI tools, here are some resources and guidelines to consider:

- The IEEE Ethically Aligned Design[25]: A Vision for Prioritizing Human Well-being with Autonomous and Intelligent Systems provides a framework for designing and developing AI systems that prioritize human well-being and ethical considerations.

- The OECD Principles on Artificial Intelligence[26]: Offers guidance on the responsible development and use of AI, focusing on issues such as transparency, accountability, and fairness.

- IBM's AI Fairness 360 toolkit[27]: Provides a set of tools and algorithms for detecting and mitigating bias in AI systems.

By familiarizing yourself with these resources and guidelines, you can develop a strong foundation in ethical AI practices and make informed decisions when selecting and using AI tools.

Remember, the responsible use of AI tools requires ongoing learning, reflection, and adaptation. As AI technologies evolve, staying informed about the latest ethical considerations and best practices is necessary. By prioritizing ethical principles and using AI tools responsibly, you can contribute to developing a more just, equitable, and beneficial AI ecosystem.

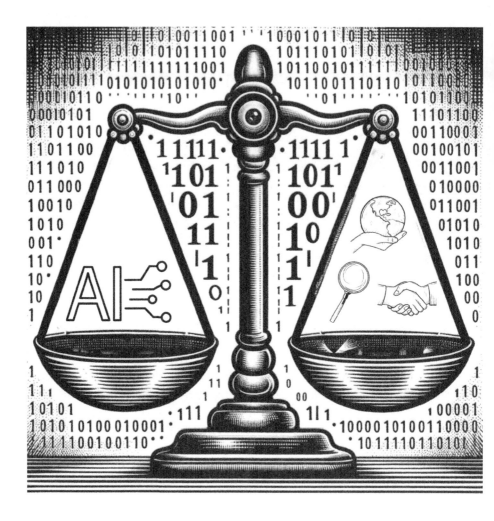

5.5 Staying Updated: How to Keep Pace with AI Advances

The field of AI is rapidly evolving, with breakthroughs, tools, and applications emerging at an unprecedented pace. As a beginner, staying updated with the latest developments in AI is key to maintaining relevant skills, identifying new opportunities, and contributing to advancing the field.

To help you stay informed and keep pace with AI advances, here are some additional strategies and resources to consider:

1. Follow AI Blogs and News Outlets:

Regularly reading AI-focused blogs and news websites can help you stay informed about the latest research, innovations, and industry trends. Some popular sources include:

- MIT Technology Review's AI section[28]

- Google AI Blog[29]

- OpenAI Blog[30]

- DeepMind Blog[31]

- AI Weekly Newsletter[32]

2. Attend AI Conferences and Workshops:

AI conferences and workshops offer opportunities to learn from experts, discover cutting-edge research, and network with professionals in the field. While some events may require travel, many now offer virtual attendance options, making them more accessible to beginners. Some notable AI conferences include:

- NeurIPS[33] (Neural Information Processing Systems)

- ICML[34] (International Conference on Machine Learning)

- AAAI[35] (Association for the Advancement of Artificial Intelligence)

3. Follow AI Thought Leaders and Researchers:

Following prominent AI thought leaders, researchers, and practitioners on social media and their blogs can provide valuable insights into the latest developments and discussions in the field. Some notable figures to follow include:

- Andrew Ng[36]

- Yann LeCun[37]

- Geoffrey Hinton[38]

- Fei-Fei Li[39]

- Andrej Karpathy[40]

4. Explore AI Research Papers and Preprints:

Reading research papers and preprints can help you stay informed about the latest scientific advances in AI. While some papers may be highly technical, many authors provide abstracts and summaries that can help beginners grasp key ideas and implications of their work. Some popular platforms for accessing AI research papers include:

- arXiv[41]

- IEEE Xplore[42]

- ACM Digital Library[43]

5. Participate in AI Projects and Competitions:

Engaging in practical AI projects and competitions can help you apply your knowledge, learn new skills, and stay motivated. Platforms like Kaggle and DrivenData offer a wide range of AI competitions and projects, allowing you to collaborate with others, benchmark your skills, and contribute to real-world applications.

By incorporating these strategies and resources into your learning journey, you can stay updated with the latest AI advances and position yourself for success in this rapidly evolving field.

Remember, staying updated with AI advances is an ongoing process that requires dedication, curiosity, and a willingness to learn. As you engage with the AI community and explore new resources, be sure to pace yourself, focus on topics that align with your goals and interests, and don't hesitate to ask questions and seek guidance from more experienced practitioners.

In addition to staying informed about the latest AI advances, it's equally important to develop a strong foundation in the fundamental concepts and techniques that underpin the field. By building a solid understanding of the core principles of AI, you'll be better equipped to evaluate new developments, identify meaningful trends, and offer meaningful contributions.

As you navigate the rapidly changing landscape of AI, remember to approach new ideas and technologies with a critical and ethical mindset. Consider the potential implications and consequences of AI advances, and strive to use your knowledge and skills in a way that promotes the responsible and beneficial development of these powerful tools.

Ultimately, staying updated with AI advances is not just about acquiring new knowledge and skills; it's about actively participating in the AI community, contributing to the discourse, and shaping the field's future direction. By staying informed, engaged, and committed to continuous learning, you can position yourself at the forefront of this exciting and transformative domain, ready to tackle the challenges and opportunities that lie ahead.

In conclusion, this chapter has provided an overview of the essential AI tools and resources that every beginner should know, including popular libraries, frameworks, and platforms for machine learning, deep learning, computer vision, and natural language processing. We've also explored strategies for leveraging free resources for self-learning, understanding AI algorithms without coding, using AI responsibly and ethically, and staying updated with the latest advances in the field.\

In the next chapter, we will finally put theory into practice. We will be using the tools and resources discussed in this chapter and putting them to work to create your very own AI projects.

---

1. https://www.tensorflow.org/

2. https://pytorch.org/

3. https://scikit-learn.org/stable/

4. https://keras.io/

5. https://opencv.org/

6. https://www.nltk.org/

7. https://spacy.io/

8. https://huggingface.co/

9. https://www.coursera.org/browse/data-science/machine-learning

10. https://developers.google.com/machine-learning/crash-course

11. https://learning.edx.org/course/course-v1:Microsoft+DAT263x+2T2018/home

12. https://machinelearningmastery.com/

13. https://towardsdatascience.com/

14. https://www.analyticsvidhya.com/

15. https://amzn.to/3XrGAbx

16. https://amzn.to/3xpTTif

17. https://amzn.to/45ALWna

18. https://www.kaggle.com/

19. https://stackoverflow.com/

20. https://www.reddit.com/r/MachineLearning/?rdt=33340

21. https://www.linkedin.com/search/results/groups/?keywords=artificial%20intelligence&sid=*2g

22. https://playground.tensorflow.org/

23. https://distill.pub/

24. https://poloclub.github.io/ganlab/

25. https://standards.ieee.org/wp-content/uploads/import/documents/other/ead_v2.pdf

26. https://www.oecd.org/digital/artificial-intelligence/

27. https://aif360.res.ibm.com/

28. https://www.technologyreview.com/topic/artificial-intelligence/

29. https://ai.google/discover/blogs/

30. https://openai.com/news/

31. https://deepmind.google/

32. https://ai-weekly.ai/newsletters/

33. https://neurips.cc/

34. https://icml.cc/

35. https://aaai.org/conference/aaai/

36. https://www.andrewng.org/

37. https://x.com/ylecun

38. https://scholar.google.com/citations?hl=en&user=JicYPdAAAAAJ

39. https://www.linkedin.com/in/fei-fei-li-4541247/

40. https://karpathy.ai/

41. https://arxiv.org/search/cs?query=Artificial+Intelligence&searchtype=all&abstracts

42. https://ieeexplore.ieee.org/Xplore/home.jsp

43. https://dl.acm.org/

Make a Difference with Your Review

Unlock the Power of Generosity

"The best way to find yourself is to lose yourself in the service of others." - *Mahatma Gandhi.*

When you help others without expecting anything in return, amazing things happen. You feel happier, more fulfilled, and even more successful. So, if we've got a chance to do that while learning about AI together, you bet I'm gonna give it a shot!

To make that happen, I've got a question for you...

Would you lend a helping hand to someone you've never met, even if they never knew it was you?

This person is a lot like you. They might be just starting out with AI, eager to learn, and looking for guidance but not quite sure where to begin.

Our mission is to make AI for Beginners accessible to everyone. It's the driving force behind everything we do. But, the only way we can truly achieve that mission is by reaching...well...everyone.

That's where you come in. Most people do judge a book by its cover (and its reviews). So, here's my request on behalf of an AI newbie you've never met:

Please help that AI beginner by leaving this book a review.

Your review won't cost you a penny and will take less than a minute, but it can change a fellow AI learner's life forever. Your review could help...

...one more student discover a passion for AI.

...one more teacher bring AI to their classroom.

...one more developer create an AI-powered app.

...one more entrepreneur launch an AI startup.

...one more dream become a reality.

To get that warm, fuzzy feeling and really help this person out, all you have to do is (and it takes less than 60 seconds)...

Leave a review.

Simply scan the QR code below to share your thoughts:

[https://www.amazon.com/review/review-your-purchases/?asin=B0D8Z1KL4M]

If you feel good about helping an anonymous AI learner, you're definitely one of us. Welcome to the club!

I'm even more excited to help you understand and apply AI in ways you never thought possible. You're going to love the projects we'll dive into in the next chapter.

Thank you from the bottom of my heart. Now, back to our regularly scheduled programming!

- Your biggest fan, Alex Bennett

P.S. Fun fact: When you help someone out, it makes you even more awesome in their eyes. If you think this book will help another AI rookie and you want to spread the love, send a copy their way!

P.P.S. Take a screenshot of your review, send it to globalinkpublishing@gmail.com, and receive a unique code to get any future books from Global Ink for FREE! It's a win-win!

Chapter 6

Hands-On Projects with AI

T heory comes to life through practical application. This chapter offers a series of hands-on, beginner-friendly AI projects designed to reinforce your understanding and showcase AI in action. From developing a simple chatbot to creating an AI-powered personal assistant, these projects provide step-by-step guidance, even for those with no prior coding experience. This practical approach will help solidify your grasp of AI concepts and their real-world applications. So, let's get our hands digital and start with your very first chatbot project.

6.1 Creating Your First Chatbot

Chatbots are computer programs that simulate human conversation through text or voice commands. They use natural language processing (NLP) and machine learning techniques to understand user input and provide relevant responses. Chatbots are widely used in customer service, e-commerce, and other industries to provide instant assistance, answer frequently asked questions, and guide users through processes.

For example, an e-commerce business can use a chatbot to handle common customer inquiries about product availability, shipping times, and return policies. Answering these FAQs frees up human support agents to focus on more complex issues, improving overall efficiency and customer satisfaction. Chatbots can also be used for lead generation, guiding potential customers through the sales funnel and providing personalized recommendations based on their preferences.

In this project, you will create a simple chatbot using Dialogflow. Dialogflow is a user-friendly, cloud-based platform that allows you to create conversational interfaces for websites, mobile applications, and messaging platforms without needing extensive programming knowledge.

Step-by-step guide:

1. Sign up for a free account on the Dialogflow website (https://dialogflow.cloud. google.com/).

2. Click the "Create Agent" button to start a new chatbot project.

3. Give your chatbot a name and set the default language.

4. Create intents for your chatbot. Intents represent the various purposes or goals of a conversation. For example, a "Greeting" intent would recognize phrases like "Hello" or "Hi" and provide an appropriate response.

5. Add training phrases representing what users might say for each intent. Dialogflow uses these phrases to understand user inputs and match them to the appropriate intent.

6. Define responses for each intent. These are the messages your chatbot will send back to the user when the intent is triggered.

7. Test your chatbot using the built-in console to ensure it responds correctly to different user inputs.

8. Use Dialogflow's integration options to integrate your chatbot with your desired platform, such as a website or messaging service.

9. Monitor your chatbot's performance and user interactions to identify areas for improvement. Based on user feedback, continuously refine your intents, training phrases, and responses.

By completing this project, you will gain hands-on experience designing and implementing a simple chatbot using a no-code platform. You'll learn how to define intents, train your chatbot, and provide appropriate responses to user queries. This project will give you a foundation in conversational AI and its applications in various domains.

6.2 An Introduction to AI with Scratch for Non-Coders

Scratch, a visual programming language developed by MIT, provides the building blocks of the coding world. It is designed with beginners in mind, especially kids, but adults find it just as fun and enlightening. It uses colorful, drag-and-drop blocks to represent coding components, allowing you to build programs without typing a single line of code. Think of it as creating a storyboard where each block is a part of your story, and you're the director who decides what happens next.

Using Scratch for AI projects is like dipping your toes in the ocean of AI without worrying about the complexities of syntax errors or complicated algorithms. It's a playground where you can experiment with basic AI concepts. For instance, you can create a simple game where characters learn from the players' inputs. Imagine designing a game where a cat learns to navigate a maze to find its food. Each time you play, the cat gets smarter, learning from the paths you guide it through. This is a basic form of machine learning, and with Scratch, you're making it happen with just a few clicks and drags.

Let's discuss some simple AI projects you can dive into using Scratch. You could start with an AI-based quiz game. Here, you create a character that asks questions, and, based on the answers given by the player, it learns to adjust the difficulty level of subsequent questions. Or a more visually engaging project where you teach a sprite (a character in Scratch) to follow objects around the screen based on simple rules you set. These projects aren't just about having fun; they're your first steps in understanding how AI works in an interactive, hands-on way.

Step-by-step guide:

1. Visit the Scratch website (https://scratch.mit.edu/) and click the "Start Creating" button to access the online editor.

2. Familiarize yourself with the Scratch interface, including the block palette, sprite editor, and stage area.

3. Create a new sprite for your AI-based quiz game character.

4. Use the "Events" and "Control" blocks to create a script that starts the game when the green flag is clicked.

5. Use the "Sensing" and "Operators" blocks to create a script that asks the player questions and checks if the answer is correct.

6. Use variables to keep track of the player's score and the difficulty level of the questions.

7. Use the "Data" and "Operators" blocks to create a script that adjusts the difficulty level based on the player's performance. For example, the difficulty level increases if the player answers three questions correctly in a row.

8. Test your game and refine the learning algorithm based on user feedback and observations.

9. Share your project with the Scratch community and explore other AI-related projects for inspiration and learning.

Completing this project will give you practical experience applying basic AI concepts using a visual programming language. You'll learn how to create interactive projects, implement simple learning algorithms, and explore the potential of AI in game development. This project serves as a foundation for understanding AI principles. It can be a stepping stone to more advanced AI projects in the future.

6.3 AI-Powered Personal Assistant with Zapier

Personal assistants help individuals organize tasks, manage schedules, and automate repetitive processes. With the power of AI and automation tools like Zapier, you can create a personalized assistant that caters to your specific needs and preferences. Zapier is a user-friendly automation platform that allows you to connect various apps and services, creating automated workflows called "Zaps." These Zaps can be triggered by specific events or actions, enabling you to automate tasks without writing any code.

For example, a busy professional can use an AI-powered personal assistant to automatically organize and prioritize their emails, schedule meetings, and send reminders for important deadlines. The assistant can learn from the user's behavior and preferences to provide more accurate and timely suggestions, helping the user stay on top of their tasks and focus on high-value activities.

In this project, you will build a simple AI-powered personal assistant using Zapier to automate a repetitive task or workflow.

Step-by-step guide:

1. Sign up for a free account on the Zapier platform (https://zapier.com/).

2. Identify a repetitive task or workflow you want to automate. For example, save attachments from incoming emails to a specific folder in your cloud storage.

3. Choose the apps or services you want to connect, such as your email provider (e.g., Gmail) and cloud storage service (e.g., Google Drive).

4. Create a new Zap by clicking the "Make a Zap" button in your Zapier dashboard.

5. Set up the trigger for your Zap. In this example, choose your email provider as the trigger app and select "New Attachment" as the trigger event.

6. Set up the action for your Zap. Choose your cloud storage service as the action app and select "Upload File" as the action event.

7. Map the information from the trigger (email attachment) to the action (upload file). Specify the folder where you want the attachments to be saved.

8. Test your Zap to ensure it works as intended. Send an email with an attachment to the connected email account and verify that the attachment is saved in the designated folder.

9. Activate your Zap and let it run automatically in the background. Whenever you receive an email with an attachment, Zapier will save the attachment to your cloud storage, saving you time and effort.

Can you believe it is this easy to start integrating AI into your daily life? You have yet to use a single line of code. However, you are already three projects deep into making your life and business/work output more productive and, thus, more fruitful.

Using Zapier gives you valuable experience using a no-code automation platform to create an AI-powered personal assistant. You'll learn how to identify tasks suitable for automation, connect different apps and services, and set up automated workflows. This project will demonstrate the power of AI and automation in streamlining daily tasks and boosting productivity.

6.4 AI for Your Personal Finance Management

Managing personal finances is crucial for achieving financial stability and reaching long-term goals. AI-powered tools can help individuals track expenses, create budgets, and make informed financial decisions. In this project, you'll create a simple

AI-powered expense tracker using Clarifai, a no-code AI platform that allows you to train and deploy computer vision models, and Zapier, a no-code automation platform that connects various apps and services.

By leveraging Clarifai's image recognition capabilities, you'll build a model that can automatically categorize expenses based on receipt images. You'll then use Zapier to connect your AI model with a Google Sheets spreadsheet, creating an automated workflow that records your expense data without requiring any coding skills.

This project demonstrates how AI can be applied to personal finance management, even without extensive technical knowledge. It showcases the potential of AI in helping individuals take control of their finances and work towards their financial goals.

Step-by-step guide:

1. Sign up for a free account on the Clarifai platform (https://www.clarifai.com/). Clarifai offers a free tier that includes 5,000 API calls per month, which is sufficient for this project.

2. Once you're logged in, create a new application by clicking on the "Create App" button. Within your new application, create a dataset by clicking on the "Datasets" tab and then "Create Dataset." Name your dataset something like "Expense Receipts."

3. Collect a set of receipt images for various expense categories, such as groceries, dining, entertainment, and utilities. Aim to have at least 10-20 images per category. Upload your receipt images to the dataset by clicking on the "Upload" button and selecting the images from your computer. Tag each image with the appropriate expense category.

4. Once your dataset is prepared, navigate to the "Models" tab and click on "Create Model." Choose "Visual Classifier" as the model type and give your model a name. Train your model using the uploaded dataset. Clarifai will use the tagged receipt images to learn patterns and features associated with each expense category.

5. After the training is complete, test your model by uploading a new receipt image and see if it correctly predicts the expense category.

6. If you have not done so for the previous project in Chapter 6.3, sign up for a free account on Zapier (https://zapier.com/). If you already have an account, just log in to your existing one.

7. Create a new Google Sheets spreadsheet to store your expense data. Set up columns for the date, expense category, and amount.

8. In Zapier, create a new Zap that triggers when a new prediction is made in Clarifai. Set up the action step in Zapier to add a new row to your Google Sheets spreadsheet. Map the expense category predicted by Clarifai to the corresponding column in your spreadsheet.

9. Test your Zap to ensure that it correctly records the expense data in your Google Sheets spreadsheet when you upload a new receipt image to Clarifai.

10. Whenever you make a purchase, take a picture of the receipt and upload it to your Clarifai application. The AI model will analyze the image, predict the expense category, and automatically add a new row to your Google Sheets spreadsheet via the Zapier integration.

By completing this project, you'll gain practical experience in creating an AI-powered expense tracker using no-code platforms like Clarifai and Zapier. You'll learn how to train a computer vision model to categorize expenses based on receipt images and automate the process of recording expense data in a spreadsheet.

To further enhance your expense tracker, consider exploring additional features in Google Sheets, such as creating charts and graphs to visualize your spending patterns or setting up budget alerts using conditional formatting. You can also expand your dataset with more diverse receipt images and fine-tune your Clarifai model for improved accuracy.

This project is another example of just how effortlessly you can start using AI to benefit you. By completing it, you'll learn how AI can automate expense tracking, provide personalized insights, and support informed financial decision-making. This project will demonstrate the potential of AI in helping individuals take control of their finances and work towards their financial goals.

6.5 Developing an AI-Powered Blog Content Idea Generator

Have you ever found yourself staring blankly at the computer screen, hoping for divine inspiration for your next blog post, getting nothing but crickets? But what if you had a clever tool that could spark ideas and spit out content suggestions like a creative whirlwind? Enter the world of AI-powered content idea generators. These tools use the power of artificial intelligence to churn out content ideas so you can save your brainpower for crafting those killer posts.

The core of using AI to generate content ideas lies in its ability to analyze existing content, identify trends, and suggest new angles you might not have considered. This digital muse can help you brainstorm topics that are likely to resonate with your readers, keeping you ahead of the curve in your niche.

Now, let's explore Metatext, a user-friendly AI writing assistant that can help you generate content ideas and even assist in the writing process. Metatext is designed to be accessible for AI beginners while offering powerful features for content creation.

Step-by-step guide:

1. Sign up for a Metatext account at https://metatext.ai/login(they offer a free trial even though it doesn't say it. Just log in, and it will create an account for you that is free to use).

2. Once logged in, navigate to the "Create" section.

3. To generate blog post ideas, use the "Blog Ideas" template. Input your blog's niche or main topic.

4. Metatext will generate a list of potential blog post ideas based on your input.

5. Review the generated ideas and select the most promising ones for your blog.

6. For each selected idea, you can use Metatext's "Blog Outline" template to create a structure for your post.

7. To flesh out your content, use the "Blog Section" template to generate paragraphs for each section of your outline.

8. Review and edit the AI-generated content, adding your own insights, examples, and unique voice.

9. Use Metatext's "Blog Title" template to generate catchy titles for your posts.

10. Repeat this process regularly to keep your content pipeline full of fresh ideas.

While AI can provide a base or an idea, the core of your content should always be uniquely yours. Think of Metatext as a brainstorming partner. It can suggest topics and even help with the initial draft, but the final post—the one that carries your signature style—should be all yours.

Moreover, transparency regarding AI use is crucial. As AI-generated content becomes more common, readers value honesty about the tools behind the content they consume. It builds trust and credibility, showing that while you use AI for ideation and assistance, the insights and opinions are genuinely yours.

An AI-powered blog content idea generator like Metatext can transform how you plan and execute your blogging strategy. It's about leveraging technology to enhance creativity, not replace it. The beauty of Metatext lies in its ability to not only generate ideas but also assist throughout the content creation process, making it a valuable tool for bloggers at any level.

So, why not give it a try? You might find yourself wondering how you ever managed without this AI-powered writing assistant. It could be the key to unlocking a wealth of engaging content ideas, streamlining your writing process, and keeping your blog fresh and relevant in today's fast-paced digital landscape.

Remember, the goal is to use AI as a tool to augment your creativity, not to rely on it entirely. Your unique perspective and expertise are what will ultimately make your content stand out. Metatext and similar AI tools are there to help you overcome writer's block, generate new ideas, and perhaps even challenge your thinking – but the final touch, the human element that connects with your readers, that's all you.

6.6 Building a Basic Image Classifier with Teachable Machine

Image classification is a common task in computer vision, where the goal is to assign labels or categories to images based on their content. It has numerous applications, such as organizing photo collections, moderating user-generated content, or identifying objects in real-time. In this project, you will build a basic image classifier using a platform called Teachable Machine.

Teachable Machine is a user-friendly, web-based tool developed by Google that allows you to create custom machine-learning models without writing code. It provides a visual interface for training image classification models using your own labeled images.

For example, a social media manager can use an image classifier to automatically categorize user-generated content based on its subject matter, such as identifying posts related to a specific product, event, or theme. This can help streamline content moderation, improve content discovery, and enable targeted marketing campaigns based on visual themes.

Step-by-step guide:

1. Visit the Teachable Machine website (https://teachablemachine.withgoogle.com /) and click "Get Started."

2. Select "Image Project" to create a new image classification model.

3. Prepare a dataset of images for each class or category you want your model to recognize. For example, if you're building a model to classify different types of animals, gather separate sets of images for cats, dogs, birds, etc.

4. Upload your image datasets to Teachable Machine by clicking each class's "Upload" button. You can also use the "Webcam" option to capture images directly from your computer's camera.

5. Train your model by clicking the "Train Model" button. Teachable Machine will use the provided images to learn the visual features and patterns that distinguish each class.

6. test your model using the "Preview" option once the training is complete. Upload new images or use your webcam to see how well the model classifies them.

7. If necessary, refine your model by adding more images to the training dataset or adjusting the model's settings. Teachable Machine allows you to control the model's complexity and learning rate.

8. When satisfied with your model's performance, click the "Export Model" button to download it in your preferred format (e.g., TensorFlow.js, TensorFlow Lite, or Keras).

9. Use the exported model in your own projects or applications. You can integrate it into websites, mobile apps, or IoT devices to classify new images based on the classes you defined during training.

If you would like to understand the workings of deep neural networks, these are the layers behind the classifier; you can watch a visual explanation here:[1] https://yout u.be/yg4Gs5_pebY&list=UULFTiWJJhaH6BviSWKLJUM9sgI highly recommend you watch the entire Image Classification Tutorial Series.

Completing this project will give you practical experience in preparing image datasets, training a model, and evaluating its performance. This project will provide a computer vision foundation and demonstrate AI's potential in automating image recognition tasks.

As you explore the exciting world of AI through these hands-on projects, remember that the key to success lies in experimentation, iteration, and continuous learning. Don't be afraid to tinker with different settings, try new ideas, and learn from your mistakes. Each project is an opportunity to deepen your understanding of AI and its practical applications.

Moreover, as you work on these projects, remember the broader implications of AI in our daily lives. From automating tasks and enhancing productivity to providing personalized recommendations and enabling creative expression, AI has the potential to transform the way we live and work. By gaining hands-on experience with AI tools and platforms, you'll be better equipped to navigate this evolving landscape and harness the power of AI. You will be able to use it for your own benefits, whether financial, personal, or business-related, but also to bring advancements to those around you and perhaps even humanity as a whole.

So, dive in, get your hands dirty, and let your creativity guide you. The world of AI is vast and full of possibilities, and these projects are just the beginning of your journey. As you continue to learn and explore, you'll find endless opportunities to apply AI innovatively and make a meaningful impact in your personal and professional life. Happy coding and happy exploring!

The next chapter will delve into AI's transformative impact on various industries, exploring how these technologies are reshaping the way we work, communicate, and innovate. From healthcare and finance to transportation and entertainment, we'll examine real-world applications of AI and discuss the opportunities and challenges that arise as these technologies become increasingly integrated into our daily lives. So, let's continue our exploration of the fascinating world of AI and discover how these powerful tools are driving progress and shaping the future.

---

1. https://youtu.be/yg4Gs5_pebY&list=UULFTiWJJhaH6BviSWKLJUM9sg

Chapter 7

The Future of Work with AI

I magine standing at the edge of a diving board, looking down into the sparkling pool of the future workforce—a pool swirled with the currents of AI. Jumping in can seem daunting, but you've got your floaties, which, in this case, are your newfound understanding of AI and its impact on jobs. Let's splash right in and explore how AI is reshaping the job landscape, transforming how we work, where, and what work we do.

7.1 AI and the Future of Jobs: What to Expect

As AI technology advances, various industries face shifts as AI becomes more integral to their operations. Sectors such as manufacturing, transport, and customer service are already seeing significant changes as AI automates routine tasks, from factory assembly lines to chat support on websites. But it's not just about robots taking over mundane tasks; it's also about creating new roles. Think about the rise of AI ethics officers and robot trainers—jobs that hardly existed a decade ago. These roles are part of the new brigade, ensuring that as machines learn to take on more tasks, they do so responsibly and efficiently.

Before you start worrying that AI is here to steal all our jobs, let's take a closer look. Yes, automation will replace some jobs, and it has already begun to do so. But history shows that technology has been a net creator of jobs. The key lies in adaptation. AI is poised to generate employment in tech-driven areas while transforming existing jobs. For instance, data analysts, AI specialists, and AI-integrated healthcare providers are in rising demand. However, we also need to be honest that not all sectors will experience this boom—jobs that involve repetitive tasks or low decision-making may decrease. But with every door that closes, a window opens. The trick is to find that window.

As the job landscape morphs under the influence of AI, so do the skills required to navigate this new terrain. The workforce must become tech-savvy—not necessarily coding wizards, but at least comfortable around digital technologies. Soft skills like problem-solving, critical thinking, and adaptability are becoming incredibly valuable. As AI handles more predictable tasks, human creativity and strategic thinking become evident, making routine workers critical thinkers and innovators. This shift emphasizes the need for continuous skill enhancement and adaptability—the ability to learn, unlearn, and relearn.

So, how do you prepare for a workplace where your co-worker might be an algorithm? First, as mentioned throughout this book, embrace lifelong learning. The notion of studying once and working for decades on the same knowledge is as outdated as floppy disks. Online courses, workshops, and self-learning platforms must become your new best friends. Stay informed about AI developments in your field and explore how they could impact your role. Also, consider lateral moves within your industry if this is likely to expand as AI grows. For example, if you're a customer service representative, consider transitioning into a role involving training and monitoring AI-powered chatbots, as this area will likely see significant growth. Building a diverse skill set that includes technical know-how and strong interpersonal skills can make you invaluable in a tech-driven job market.

Are You Prepared for an AI-Driven Workplace?

Answer the questions below to determine your readiness to adapt to the AI-transformed job market. Your answers will help you identify areas where you need to improve your skills or knowledge.

1. How comfortable are you with using digital tools and platforms?

2. Do you regularly update yourself on your industry's latest technologies and trends?

3. How often do you learn new skills that are not directly related to your current job?

If your answers aren't "Very, "Yes," and "Often," then you've got some work to do. Hit the books and the web, or start playing with projects like the ones mentioned in Chapter 6 to gear up for the future AI workforce. Remember, staying curious and proactive is half the battle won.

7.2 Upskilling for an AI World: Essential Skills for the Future

Let's face it: the AI train has not only left the station, but it's picking up speed. And in this rapidly changing landscape, clinging to old skill sets is about as effective as trying to text with a rotary phone. What you need is a robust set of skills that are as future-proof as possible. In an AI-driven world, these aren't just nice-to-haves but must-haves. So, what's in this essential toolkit for the future? Technical skills, critical thinking, and creativity top the list.

Technical prowess doesn't mean you need to be the next tech billionaire, but a basic understanding of how AI and technology function will not hurt. It's about getting comfortable with the tech terminology and tools that are becoming the backbone of nearly every industry. From understanding data analytics to grasping basic programming concepts, these skills could mean the difference between leading the charge and playing catch-up.

Then there's critical thinking -- your secret weapon in a world awash with data. With AI churning out information at warp speed, the ability to analyze, evaluate, and make pin-sharp decisions is more valuable than ever. It's like being a detective in a crime show; you need to sift through the noise to find the clues that matter. This skill ensures you are not just a passive consumer of AI outputs but an active, discerning participant in the AI process.

And let's not forget creativity. In the automation age, creativity is the golden ticket. It's what machines can't replicate (at least not yet). Whether it's coming up with innovative solutions to complex problems or thinking up a new product that revolutionizes the market, creativity ensures you stay relevant and irreplaceable.

How do you acquire these skills? Thankfully, the resources are as plentiful as cat videos on the internet. There are online courses galore -- from platforms like Coursera and Udacity that offer courses designed by industry experts and top universities to specialized boot camps like General Assembly, which immerse you in intensive, practical learning experiences. Whether you want a deep dive into AI programming or a crash course in digital marketing, there's something out there to fit your schedule, learning style, and interests.

Self-study materials are also invaluable. Books such as this one, podcasts, and tutorial videos can supplement formal courses, allowing you to learn at your own pace. For instance, if you're intrigued by AI ethics, why not grab a book like "Weapons of Math Destruction" by Cathy O'Neil? It's a fantastic read that explores how big data increases inequality and threatens democracy. Resources like these enhance your understanding and spark ideas for applying AI in ethical, impactful ways.

The role of traditional education institutions is also evolving in this context. Universities and colleges are increasingly integrating AI and technology-focused modules into their curricula. But more than that, they're fostering partnerships with tech companies and startups to provide students real-world experience and insights. These collaborations help bridge the gap between academic knowledge and industry needs, ensuring that when you step out of the ivory tower, you're theoretically prepared and practically ready to tackle the challenges of an AI-driven workplace.

Adaptability is another skill that's becoming vital. In an era where change is the only constant, being able to pivot and adapt is invaluable. This means staying curious, being open to new ideas, and continuously updating your skills. Think of it like software updates for your phone; things start to glitch without them. The same goes for your skill set in an AI-powered world.

So, remember, upskilling for an AI world isn't a one-and-done deal. It's an ongoing process that requires you to stay active, engaged, and perpetually ready to learn. Whether beefing up your tech skills, honing your critical thinking, or letting your creativity run wild, the goal is to keep your toolkit sharp and your mind sharper. With these skills in your arsenal, you're not just ready for the future; you're ready to shape it.

7.3 AI Entrepreneurship: Starting Your AI-Driven Business

Now that you've gained some confidence in the world and application of AI, you might be considering dipping your toes into the entrepreneurial waters of AI. Fantastic! AI entrepreneurship is not just bursting with opportunities; it's a real treasure trove for the innovative mind. With sectors ranging from agriculture, where AI can optimize crop yields and resource management, to public infrastructure, where AI can transform how we monitor and maintain our cities, the potential areas for injecting some AI magic are vast and varied. Picture this: your startup could be the next big thing in providing AI-driven solutions for sustainable farming or developing intelligent systems that enhance the efficiency and safety of our urban spaces.

But let's keep it real; starting an AI-driven business isn't just about having a groundbreaking idea. It's about navigating a labyrinth of challenges unique to the high-tech world of AI. Think about the ethical implications of your AI products—could they inadvertently become biased? Are they infringing on privacy? These are the modern-day monsters under the bed of any AI entrepreneur. Then, there's the maze of data privacy regulations. With legislation like GDPR in Europe and various others around the globe, you need to be as savvy about legal requirements as you are about coding algorithms.

Moreover, each AI venture comes with its own set of technical challenges. Ensuring your AI systems are not just intelligent but also scalable and reliable can feel like trying to solve a Rubik's cube blindfolded. And let's not forget the need for substantial data to train your algorithms. Securing this data, ensuring its quality and diversity, and handling the data responsibly are pivotal tasks that can make or break your AI application.

I want to share some thrilling success stories to fuel your entrepreneurial fire. Take the story of a small startup that began with the idea of using AI to optimize energy use in commercial buildings. With a genius blend of IoT devices and AI analytics, they provided a solution that not only cut costs but also significantly reduced their clients' carbon footprint. Their success was in crafting a stellar product and their strategic partnerships with energy consultants and property managers, showcasing the importance of understanding your industry's ecosystem.

Another inspiring tale comes from the healthcare sector, where a visionary team used AI to enhance early diagnosis of neurological disorders. They faced a mountain of challenges, from ensuring the accuracy and ethical handling of medical data to gaining the trust of medical professionals. However, their commitment to continuous learning and adaptation allowed them to create a tool that supported doctors and provided immense value to patients, illustrating the profound impact AI can have on lives.

Knowing where to look for resources can be your golden ticket if you're all fired up and ready to turn your AI dream into reality. First, the financial runway: securing funding is paramount. Look into AI-specific venture capital firms keen on supporting disruptive AI technologies. These firms not only provide capital but can also offer valuable guidance and industry connections, which is imperative for young startups.

For those at the idea stage, accelerators and incubators can be invaluable. Programs like Techstars AI and Y Combinator offer mentorship, investment, and access to a network of tech experts and entrepreneurs. These environments are perfect for refining your business model, developing your product, and preparing for pitches to prominent investors.

Moreover, don't underestimate the power of community support. Engaging with online forums, attending AI meetups, and participating in hackathons can provide inspiration, practical insights, and potential collaborations. Platforms like Meetup. com or professional groups on LinkedIn offer avenues to connect with like-minded individuals who can share their experiences, advice, and warnings about possible pitfalls.

While the path of AI entrepreneurship is fraught with challenges, it is also ripe with opportunities for those willing to tackle the complexities of modern technology while keeping an ethical compass and a clear vision. Whether revolutionizing an existing industry or creating a new market niche, the key lies in persistent learning, adapting swiftly, and embracing the thrilling uncertainties of the AI frontier. As you forge ahead, equip yourself with the right tools, surround yourself with experts, and keep your eyes on the transformative potential of your AI venture.

7.4 AI in Creative Industries: New Roles and Opportunities

From the rhythmic beats of music to the evocative strokes of a painter's brush, AI is nudging the boundaries and stretching them in ways that promise an explosion of creativity across industries. Integrating AI within art, music, and writing is not just altering the landscape; it's creating a new one filled with novel roles and boundless opportunities.

For instance, AI is tuning up to be a game-changer in the music industry. Picture this: AI algorithms that can compose music or create new sounds, giving rise to roles like AI music producers who blend traditional composition techniques with algorithmic innovation to create melodies that might have been unfathomable. These professionals aren't just working with notes and instruments; they're manipulating data and algorithms to hit those emotional chords. Meanwhile, visual arts are seeing the emergence of AI-driven design tools that can assist in creating more complex and intricate artworks. Artists are now collaborating with AI to push the envelope on what constitutes art, leading to new forms and expressions that can be personalized for the viewer in real-time.

But how about writing? Yes, that sanctuary of human emotion and expression is also feeling the AI ripple. Using natural language processing (NLP), AI-powered writing assistants help craft everything from mundane emails to compelling pieces of fiction. The role of an AI literary assistant is becoming increasingly mainstream in editing, suggesting plot twists, and even overcoming writer's block. It's like having a muse that doesn't just inspire but also contributes, making the solitary act of writing a bit more interactive.

The magic happens at the intersection of human ingenuity and AI's capabilities. Consider an artist and an AI collaborating to produce a piece of art. The artist inputs initial ideas and themes, and the AI, using its vast database, suggests modifications, adds elements based on current trends, or introduces styles from different eras. This synergy enhances creativity and democratizes art creation, making it accessible to non-artists who wish to express their creativity. The result? A fusion of human emotion and machine precision that yields genuinely unique artworks.

Similarly, in music, collaborations between AI algorithms and human musicians compose symphonies that blend genres in unprecedented ways. These projects often lead to performances where AI-generated music is played by human musicians, blurring the lines between the composer and the instrument, the creator and the creation. This partnership can be particularly potent in live performances, where AI can adapt music in real-time to audience reactions, creating an interactive experience that was once the sole domain of human intuition.

For professionals in creative fields, riding the AI wave requires a surfboard crafted from adaptability and a willingness to learn. Understanding AI tools and technologies can turn potential threats into opportunities. For instance, graphic designers might benefit from learning how AI can automate routine design aspects, freeing them up to focus on more creative and complex tasks. Workshops, online tutorials, and courses on AI applications in creative fields can provide the necessary skills and knowledge.

Staying updated with AI advancements ensures that creatives can leverage these technologies rather than be blindsided by them. Networking with other professionals exploring AI, attending industry conferences, and participating in forums can provide insights and inspiration on integrating AI into one's work effectively.

The vista is thrilling as we peer into the crystal ball to speculate on the future of creativity in an AI-driven world. AI is setting the stage for a new era of creative professions where technology enhances human creativity, making it more interactive, personalized, and accessible. However, the challenge lies in ensuring that this fusion does not stifle human creativity but rather amplifies it, allowing artists to explore new dimensions and push boundaries further.

In the grand tapestry of the creative industries, AI's threads are weaving new patterns that might initially seem alien but soon could become the new norm. As these technologies continue to evolve, they promise to redefine existing art forms and give birth to new ones, testing the limits of what we perceive as creativity. The key to thriving in this evolving landscape is a blend of curiosity, adaptability, and a relentless pursuit of creative excellence powered by both human and artificial muses.

7.5 How to Stay Relevant in an AI-Driven World

Let's face it: the AI wave isn't just coming; it's already crashing over us like a giant tech surf. Riding this wave without wiping out means embracing continuous learning as a lifestyle. Think of it as keeping your brain in perpetual beta mode, where you always update, improve, and add new features. Staying abreast of AI developments isn't just about keeping your job or staying competitive; it's about being a proactive part of the future—shaping it, not just being shaped by it.

Creating a personal learning ecosystem is your strategy for thriving in this AI-infused era. This ecosystem spans formal education—yes, those degrees and certificates still matter—and the vast ocean of online resources and the real-world experiences that provide context and practical know-how. For instance, platforms like LinkedIn Learning, Udacity, or Coursera offer courses in everything from basic programming to advanced AI applications. But don't just stop at online courses. Extend your learning into the real world by attending workshops, seminars, and industry conferences. These not only deepen your understanding but also provide networking opportunities that are crucial for staying plugged into the industry's pulse.

The cornerstone of this approach is a growth mindset, a fundamental shift in how you view your capabilities. With a growth mindset, challenges transform into opportunities. Every mistake and hiccup is a chance to learn and grow rather than a signal to give up. You might start a project using one technology, and by the time it's midway, a new tool or technique might emerge. Adapting isn't optional; it's necessary. So, when you hit a wall, don't turn around. Look for a ladder or a rope, or build your wings and climb over it.

Networking and community involvement are no longer about exchanging business cards or adding connections on LinkedIn. Instead, they are your lifeline, keeping you connected to new ideas, emerging trends, and opportunities that could bypass you in the silo of solo work. Engage actively in AI communities online and offline. Join forums where AI developments are discussed, from Reddit threads to specialized AI and machine learning groups on professional networks. Attend local meetups, participate in hackathons, or even online competitions like those on Kaggle. These interactions can lead to collaborations, job opportunities, and even friendships that make the AI journey a shared adventure rather than a solo quest.

Building this continuous learning ecosystem, embracing a growth mindset, and engaging with a community is more than setting yourself up for professional development. It's about a lifelong adventure in a field as dynamic as it is influential. AI isn't just changing the world; it's making a whole new one. So, gear up, stay curious, and dive into the learning wave. After all, in an AI-driven world, staying relevant is about learning fast and adapting even faster.

7.6 Ethical Job Displacement: Navigating AI Transitions

The term "ethical job displacement" might sound like a fancy way of saying, "Sorry, robots took your job." But more accurately, it revolves around the idea of making the transition as smooth and fair as possible. Let's face it: with AI taking on tasks ranging from scheduling meetings to diagnosing diseases, specific jobs will evolve or, in some cases, get phased out. The real kicker is ensuring that this evolution doesn't leave anyone behind, clinging to the raft of outdated skills.

What does ethical job displacement really mean? It's about acknowledging that while AI brings efficiency and innovation, it also carries the responsibility of reshaping the workforce ethically. This means that companies and governments need to think about how to help individuals transition rather than just handing them pink slips and moving on. It's like renovating your house; you wouldn't just discard all your old furniture. Some of it can be repurposed, refurbished, or donated. Likewise, workforce transitions should focus on repurposing skills, refurbishing roles, and, sometimes, helping workers transition to entirely new careers.

For businesses and policymakers, the goal is to cushion the impact of AI transitions. One effective strategy is investing in retraining programs. Think of it as updating the workforce's software. Just as you wouldn't toss out a smartphone just because it's a model behind, you shouldn't write off experienced employees without first offering them a chance to update their skills. Companies like Amazon have set precedents with their upskilling programs designed to equip their employees with skills relevant to emerging roles within the company.

Another strategy is creating safety nets. This isn't just about financial support, although that's an integral part of it. It's also about providing career counseling and job placement services to help displaced workers navigate their new roles. In some European countries, for example, job transition agencies work with companies to ensure workers have a new job lined up before their current role becomes obsolete.

If you're sitting there wondering how to steer your own boat in these choppy waters, the first step is to identify your transferable skills. These are your lifeboats, the skills that can float in any job market. Skills like problem-solving, communication, and project management are valuable everywhere. Next, explore new career paths that might interest you. This could be the perfect opportunity to dive into a field you've always been passionate about but never had the chance to pursue.

Also, keep an eye on emerging roles created by AI and technology. Roles like Virtual Reality Architect, AI-Assisted Cybersecurity Analyst, or Augmented Reality

Designer might be on the rise. By understanding where the job market currents are flowing, you can better position yourself to swim rather than sink.

Finally, reflecting on the broader societal role in ensuring ethical AI transitions is essential. It's a collective effort. Governments must enact policies encouraging companies to invest in employee retraining and support displaced workers. Educational institutions must adapt curricula to include AI and technology training at all levels. And society as a whole needs to shift its mindset to value continuous learning and adaptability.

In a world where technology is rapidly reshaping landscapes, ethical job displacement is about making sure that everyone has a map, a compass, and the right gear to navigate the new terrain. It's about assuring that the AI revolution benefits everyone technologically, economically, socially, and morally.

As we close this chapter on navigating the AI-driven changes in the workforce, remember that the future is not something we enter; it's something we create. Ethical job displacement might be a challenge, but it is also an incredible opportunity—to build a more resilient, adaptive, and inclusive workforce. Next, we'll explore how AI is reshaping specific industries, from healthcare to finance, and how these changes create new opportunities and challenges for businesses and workers alike. Stay tuned because the journey into the impact of AI on industries is about to get interesting.

Chapter 8

Advanced AI Trends and Innovations

The frontier of AI is constantly expanding, with new developments pushing the boundaries of possibility. This chapter explores cutting-edge trends and innovations shaping the future of AI. From the integration of quantum computing to AI's role in space exploration, we'll examine the technologies poised to define tomorrow's world. Additionally, we'll consider the ethical implications of these advancements, providing a balanced view of AI's potential future impact on society.

8.1 Exploring the Frontiers: Quantum Computing and AI

With all the mindblowing developments we have already discussed, is there still room for further innovations to fill us with awe? You wouldn't think so. But this is where AI got knocked up and is about to have quantum computing's baby. This baby not only thinks but also evolves, adapts, and revolutionizes everything at a breakneck speed. If quantum mechanics has always seemed like a topic reserved for physicists and mathematicians, don't worry! We'll break down these brain-bending concepts into snackable bits. So, buckle up! We're exploring how quantum computing joins AI to redefine the boundaries of technology and innovation.

Quantum computing is all about using the principles of quantum mechanics (the behavior of energy and material on the atomic and subatomic levels) to perform calculations at speeds unfathomable to traditional computers. Imagine doing a century's worth of computations in the blink of an eye. That's the playground we're talking about!

So, why does this matter to AI? Well, AI loves data. It devours it for breakfast, lunch, and dinner to make intelligent decisions. As brilliant as they are, traditional computers can only munch on so much data at once. Enter quantum computers, which can process massive datasets much faster and more efficiently due to their ability to hold and process information in a quantum state, known as qubits. AI systems can learn from larger datasets faster, becoming more accurate and more awesome.

The synergy here is like pairing wine with cheese; they enhance each other beautifully. Quantum computing raises the bar for what AI can achieve, especially in fields requiring complex simulations like molecular biology, financial modeling, or climate forecasting. For instance, in drug discovery, quantum AI can analyze vast combinations of molecular interactions at speeds impossible for current standards, potentially slashing years off the development time of new medications.

But it's more than speed. Quantum computing can also help AI tackle problems considered too complex for classical computers. Problems involving variables that change in real-time or algorithms that require simultaneous computations (think optimizing supply chains in real-time during a crisis) are just the tip of the iceberg.

Before you think quantum computers are about to pop up in every home like smart speakers, let's talk about the challenges. Quantum computing is still very much in its inception stages. These machines are incredibly delicate and need specific operating conditions, like supercool temperatures akin to outer space. They're also prone to errors due to quantum noise (unwanted disturbances that affect the state of quantum bits (qubits). This noise can arise from various sources, including interaction with the surrounding environment and temperature fluctuations.) and interference (When quantum states cancel each other out, reducing the probability of certain outcomes.).

The timeline for widespread use is still fuzzy. While we have made significant strides, and tech giants like Google and IBM are sprinting forward, we're likely a decade (if not more) away from quantum computers becoming mainstream. Meanwhile, the focus is on creating more stable qubits, enhancing error correction methods, and developing quantum algorithms that can run on these new systems.

The long-term implications of quantum-enhanced AI are as vast as the universe. We're looking at AI systems that could solve traffic congestion problems in real time, manage power grids more efficiently, or personalize education to each student's learning style and pace, all in seconds.

As we stand on this frontier, the potential of quantum computing intertwined with AI offers a peek into a future where the line between science fiction and reality blurs. The possibilities are as limitless as they are exhilarating, making this one of the most exciting spaces to watch and participate in.

8.2 The Role of AI in Combating Climate Change

Let's paint a picture where technology is more than a tool to build more ingenious gadgets. It's a means to a healthier planet. Here, Artificial Intelligence isn't just a whiz at crunching numbers and processing data—it's a green warrior in the battle against climate change. AI is doing some pretty impressive work in climate modeling. On top of telling you if you'll need an umbrella tomorrow, it can interpret complex climate systems to predict changes and prepare for future scenarios. With their ability to digest and analyze vast datasets from satellite imagery and sensors, AI models help scientists simulate and predict climate trends more accurately. For instance, they can predict how melting ice caps might affect ocean currents. More than future predictions, AI helps in real-time, too. For example, in places where bushfires are a significant hazard, AI systems analyze weather reports, historical data, and satellite imagery to predict fire outbreaks before they happen, potentially saving thousands of lives.

Moving on, let's talk about renewable energy. AI's role here is like that of a master chess player who plans five moves ahead. It optimizes how energy from renewable sources is distributed and consumed. By predicting peak times for energy use, AI systems adjust the flow from wind turbines and solar panels to ensure they meet user demand without waste. This kind of optimization not only makes renewable energy more viable but also more profitable. It's a win-win for businesses and the environment.

Deforestation, another environmental villain, is also on AI's radar. AI-driven drones and satellite monitoring systems keep an eye on forested regions, alerting agencies about illegal logging activities in real-time. This helps take swift action and potentially prevents massive ecological damage. AI doesn't stop at detection; it also helps in reforestation efforts. AI algorithms analyze soil data, climate conditions, and even the type of trees that would grow best in a particular area, guiding planting efforts that are more likely to thrive.

Let's showcase a few champions where AI has made a remarkable difference in environmental conservation. Take the story of a startup that used AI to optimize water usage in agriculture. By analyzing weather data, soil conditions, and crop types, their AI system provided farmers with precise watering schedules, reducing water usage by up to 30% while increasing crop yields. Then there's the AI program that helped a city reduce its carbon footprint by optimizing traffic flows, reducing idle time for vehicles stuck in traffic, and effectively cutting down emissions.

But it's not all sunny days and clear skies; using AI in environmental efforts comes with its share of clouds. One primary concern is the energy consumption of AI systems themselves. Training sophisticated AI models requires a lot of computational power, which can lead to significant carbon emissions. It's a bit ironic, isn't it? Using AI to save the environment also contributes to the problem. Addressing this involves using more energy-efficient hardware or powering data centers with renewable energy.

Tackling climate change is not a solo mission. It requires the collective effort of AI researchers, environmental scientists, and policymakers. Collaborative projects where tech companies partner with environmental organizations and governments can lead to innovative solutions that are both effective and sustainable. For instance, an AI tool developed in collaboration with environmental scientists can help city planners simulate various urban development scenarios and their environmental impacts before making decisions.

These partnerships accelerate the development of effective solutions and ensure they are aligned with real-world needs and grounded in scientific research. By working together, these diverse groups can also navigate the ethical and practical challenges more swiftly, ensuring that the solutions are technologically sound, socially responsible, and environmentally sustainable.

As AI continues to evolve, its role in environmental conservation appears increasingly promising. It offers new tools to combat climate change, optimize resource use, and protect our natural world. The key lies in harnessing this potential responsibly, ensuring that our tech advancements contribute positively to the planet. So, as we step further into this AI-assisted green future, let's remain vigilant, innovative, and, most importantly, collaborative.

8.3 AI in Space Exploration: Opportunities and Challenges

Let's blast off from Earth and zoom into the cosmos, where AI isn't just a helpful tool—it's an additional crew member on our journey through space. Picture this: autonomous rovers rolling over the rocky terrains of Mars, AI algorithms processing astronomical amounts of data from distant galaxies, and robotic arms fixing spacecrafts in zero gravity. And it's what's happening right now, thanks to the integration of AI in space exploration. More than sticking flags on celestial bodies, it's about deepening our understanding of the universe and potentially paving the way for future human settlements in space.

AI's role in space exploration has been transformative, especially in handling tasks that are too dangerous, mundane, or intricate for astronauts. Take the Mars rovers, for example. These robotic explorers, equipped with AI, navigate the Martian surface autonomously, deciding on the fly which paths to take and what rocks to study. This is pivotal as every minute of communication between Mars and Earth can take up to 20 minutes. So, these rovers must be good at making independent decisions without a quick check-back with their human buddies.

Besides roving on Mars, AI also processes the vast amounts of data we receive from space probes and satellites. This data includes everything from temperature readings to cosmic ray measurements, and it's far too much for human teams to analyze without some AI muscle. By sifting through this data, AI helps identify patterns and anomalies that might go unnoticed, like discovering new exoplanets that orbit stars light-years away or monitoring asteroid trajectories to keep our planet safe.

The cosmos is the limit when it comes to what AI can help us achieve in space. AI's role in crewed space missions is one of the most exciting prospects. As we dream about sending humans deeper into space—maybe to Mars or beyond—AI could be the co-pilot that makes these missions possible. It could manage life-support systems, monitor the health and well-being of astronauts, and even make real-time decisions during spacewalks or emergencies. Imagine an AI system that can diagnose and treat medical issues on the spot or one that can tweak the spacecraft's trajectory to avoid incoming space debris.

Moreover, AI's capability to run simulations is invaluable in planning missions. Before a rocket leaves the ground, AI can simulate countless scenarios to predict potential outcomes, helping scientists choose the safest and most efficient path to their destination. This reduces risks and increases the likelihood of mission success, which is essential when you're talking about the unforgiving environment of space.

Of course, deploying AI in space has its challenges. Space is a harsh and unpredictable environment, and AI systems must be incredibly robust to operate effectively. For instance, cosmic radiation poses a significant risk to the integrity of AI hardware. Unlike on Earth, where we have the atmosphere to protect us, space is a free-for-all for radiation, which can damage or disrupt electronic equipment. Developing AI systems that can withstand these conditions is a significant engineering challenge.

Data limitation is another hurdle. While it might seem like we have a lot of data about space, in the grand scheme of things, it's just a drop in the cosmic ocean. AI systems learn best from large, comprehensive datasets, and we're still gathering the basics in many areas of space exploration. This lack of data can limit the effectiveness of AI in making predictions or decisions.

Looking ahead, the potential for AI in space exploration is as boundless as the universe itself. We're talking about AI systems that could autonomously operate space stations, manage interplanetary mining operations, or even assist in terraforming planets to make them habitable for humans. As AI continues to evolve, its ability to learn and adapt could make it the perfect partner in our quest to visit and perhaps even reside in other parts of our solar system.

In the immediate future, AI could enable long-duration missions where human life might be unsustainable, such as voyages to the outer planets or detailed exploration of asteroids. These missions could help us understand more about our own planet and the risks we face from cosmic events. AI could act as our forward scouts in space, providing imperative information and paving the way for human explorers to follow.

As we continue to push the boundaries of what's possible in space exploration, AI is a fundamental tool in our cosmic toolkit. From enhancing the safety and efficacy of missions to more lofty aspirations, such as helping us find a new home among the stars, AI's role in space exploration is not just beneficial; it's essential. So, as we gaze up at the stars, let's remember that our path to them might just be paved with algorithms and AI.

8.4 The Next Wave: AI in Augmented and Virtual Reality

Imagine slipping on a VR headset and stepping into a world where you can learn surgery from a top surgeon right from your living room or donning AR glasses that overlay data about a historical site as you wander through its ruins. Does it sound like something from a futuristic movie? Well, it's rapidly becoming our reality, thanks to the fusion of AI with augmented reality (AR) and virtual reality (VR). This combo isn't just about creating cool new games or gimmicky apps; it's revolutionizing how we interact with the world and each other. AI is the secret sauce that makes AR/VR not just immersive but also brilliant, personalizing experiences in real-time and making them interactive in ways that were once pure fantasy.

At its core, AI helps these technologies understand and interact with the real world in a meaningful way. In AR, AI algorithms process data from cameras and sensors to overlay digital content onto the real world in a seamless way. It could be something as simple as showing you the fastest route to walk through a crowded city or as complex as simulating how a new piece of furniture would look in your living room under different lighting conditions. VR, on the other hand, creates an entirely immersive experience. AI makes these experiences feel real by responding to your actions and decisions, creating dynamic narratives that adapt to how you interact with the VR world.

The applications of AI-powered AR/VR are sprawling across industries. In education, imagine VR classrooms that take students on a virtual field trip to Mars or through the human bloodstream, with AI guiding the experience, answering questions, and adapting lessons to each student's pace and learning style. Healthcare is another field that is reaping the benefits of AI in AR/VR. Surgeons use AR to overlay medical imaging over their patients during procedures, enhancing precision without looking away from the surgical site. AI-powered VR simulations are used to train medical staff and improve their skills in a risk-free environment. In entertainment, AI-driven AR/VR creates more engaging, personalized content, whether altering the storyline in a virtual adventure based on your choices or recommending new VR games based on what you've enjoyed before.

However, developing these AI-driven AR/VR experiences has hurdles. Technically, integrating AI with AR/VR requires significant processing power, often more than what standard consumer devices can offer. This has led to ongoing efforts to optimize AI algorithms for efficiency without sacrificing performance. There's also the challenge of creating AI models that can quickly process and respond to vast amounts of data, ensuring that AR/VR interactions feel natural and responsive. Imagine a VR training module for firefighters that needs to simulate dynamic, changing conditions based on the trainee's actions; achieving this level of responsiveness requires incredibly sophisticated AI.

Ethically, there are significant considerations, too, especially around privacy and safety. With AR, devices can potentially collect personal data about users' surroundings without their full consent. Think about AR apps that scan and analyze your environment to provide services—where does all that data go, and who has access to it? VR also poses safety concerns, as fully immersive environments must be designed carefully to prevent physical harm to users who might not be aware of their real-world surroundings.

Looking ahead, the potential for AI in AR/VR is staggering. We're talking about fully immersive virtual environments where you can interact with AI-driven characters as complex as real humans or AR applications that can act as real-time interpreters of foreign languages as you converse with someone, overlaying subtitles in your field of vision. The key to realizing this future will lie in making AI more competent and efficient, ensuring it can handle the immense processing demands of advanced AR/VR applications without compromising user privacy or safety. As we navigate these challenges, the fusion of AI with AR and VR stands poised to redefine our perception of reality, offering new ways to learn, explore, and connect.

8.5 Ethical AI: Future Considerations for a Fairer World

As we continue to weave AI into the fabric of our daily lives, evolving ethical standards are not just niceties—they are essential to safeguarding the AI wave that lifts all boats and not just a privileged few. Ethical AI ensures that these technologies are developed and deployed in a way that reflects our collective values and morals, promoting fairness and protecting rights while steering clear of bias and discrimination.

The thing about ethics in AI is that they're not set in stone. As our societies evolve, so do our understandings of what's right and wrong—and so must our ethical frameworks for AI. This continual reassessment is crucial because what seemed okay a decade ago might not pass muster today. Think about facial recognition technology. Not long ago, it was hailed as a breakthrough in security and convenience. Fast forward to today, and we're grappling with its implications on privacy and its potential for racial profiling. Ensuring AI ethics keep pace with such shifts is like updating your phone's OS; it's about keeping it relevant and effective in addressing new challenges and contexts.

AI technologies connect and impact people worldwide, so a chorus of diverse voices should shape their guiding ethical principles. This means bringing together ethicists, scientists, policymakers, and community representatives from around the world to forge standards that reflect a wide range of cultural norms and values.

Let's talk about innovations in ethical AI. Developers are now crafting algorithms designed to detect and mitigate bias—think of them as the referees in the game of AI development. These tools assess AI systems for fairness, looking out for skewed data or biased outcomes. For instance, some algorithms are trained to recognize when a facial recognition system performs poorly with specific demographic groups, prompting developers to make necessary adjustments. Transparency is another big area of focus. New systems are being developed to track and explain decisions made by AI, kind of like a breadcrumb trail that shows how the AI came to a particular conclusion. This is important for trust and accountability, ensuring that if an AI system does mess up, we can figure out why and fix it.

Reflecting on how AI can contribute to a fairer world, it's clear that this technology has tremendous potential to address social and economic disparities. AI can help tailor educational tools to meet the needs of students from diverse backgrounds, breaking down barriers that have traditionally hindered access to quality education. AI can analyze data in healthcare to identify and address gaps in care and outcomes among different population groups, making healthcare more equitable. The trick is to guarantee that these systems are accessible to those who could benefit most, bridging rather than widening the digital divide.

As we stand on the brink of AI transforming every corner of our lives, the focus on ethical AI has never been more critical. By fostering global collaboration, pushing for innovations in fairness and transparency, and harnessing AI's potential to reduce inequalities, we can steer the AI ship toward a future that isn't just technologically advanced but is also fair and just for all. We can all leverage this powerful tool to create a world where technology champions equity and inclusivity. So, as we continue to explore and expand AI's capabilities, let's commit to keeping ethics at the heart of innovation, ensuring that the AI future we're building is one we can all look forward to and benefit from.

8.6 The Continuous Learning Machine: How AI Evolves Itself

Imagine if you could learn a new language while you sleep or master the piano without ever touching the keys. Sounds wild, right? In AI, machines are stepping up their game to something akin to this -- they're learning on their own, continuously improving without human babysitting; it's a groundbreaking shift in how AI systems evolve and adapt. These AIs, which we can think of as 'continuous learning machines,' are designed to soak up new information from their environments and experiences, tweaking themselves to perform better over time.

The concept here is straightforward but revolutionary. Traditional AI systems require humans to manually update their algorithms or feed them new data to refine their abilities. But continuous learning machines? They're the prodigies of AI, learning from ongoing data, making decisions based on new information, and even updating their own algorithms without human intervention. This means they can adapt to new situations or changes in their environment in real time. Imagine a security AI that learns to recognize new types of cyber threats as it encounters them or a healthcare AI that updates its diagnostic criteria based on the latest medical research.

Recent advancements in AI methodologies are what's powering this evolution. Take reinforcement learning, for example. This technique trains machines via trial and error, allowing them to learn from their actions. If the AI makes a choice that leads to a positive outcome, it receives a 'reward'; if not, it adjusts its approach. Picture a robot learning to navigate a maze -- each time it bumps into a wall, it learns that path is a no-go. Each time it finds a quicker route to the goal, it remembers that path for future runs.

Then there's self-supervised learning, a method where machines learn from data that hasn't been explicitly labeled or categorized by humans. This technique enables AIs to understand and process vast amounts of data that are too complex or too costly for humans to annotate. For instance, AI used in natural language processing can learn to understand nuances and contexts of new languages or dialects by analyzing extensive text collections without needing detailed explanations from linguists.

However, let's repeat this one more time- with great power comes great responsibility -- and, in the case of AI, great complexity. One of the biggest challenges with continuous learning machines is ensuring they don't veer off course. Without constant human oversight, there's a risk that these AIs might develop unintended behaviors or biases based on flawed data or malicious inputs. Think about an AI that starts with a slight bias and then continues to learn in a way that amplifies that bias over time, leading to increasingly skewed decisions.

The ethical implications are substantial. How do we ensure these systems adhere to ethical guidelines if they evolve independently? Establishing robust frameworks for AI behavior, continuous monitoring systems, and fail-safes is fundamental to preventing and correcting potential deviations that could lead to harmful outcomes.

Looking ahead, the potential of continuous learning machines is both exciting and daunting. On one hand, they could vastly increase the efficiency and applicability of AI across sectors—from real-time personalized learning models that evolve with students' educational needs to dynamic environmental systems that adjust to live climate data. On the other hand, the autonomy of these systems raises significant questions about control, oversight, and safety.

As we integrate these ever-learning AIs into more aspects of daily life, we must balance their potential benefits with the risks they pose. Ensuring these technologies are developed with an eye for safety, ethics, and transparency will be key to harnessing their capabilities responsibly. As we venture further into this new era of AI, it's clear that our approach to designing, monitoring, and integrating these systems will need to be as adaptive and intelligent as the technologies themselves.

In wrapping up this exploration into the realm of self-evolving AI, we've peeked into a future where machines not only learn but also adapt by themselves, continuously improving and evolving. This glimpse into what lies ahead not only expands our understanding of the potential and challenges of advanced AI systems but also underscores the importance of steering these developments with careful consideration and foresight.

Conclusion

Well, here we are at the end of our grand tour through the world of Artificial Intelligence. What a ride it's been, from deciphering the basics of AI to diving deep into the quantum leaps AI is destined to make. If you've felt like you've been in a whirlwind of data, algorithms, and futuristic predictions, you're not alone. My goal was to take you from a place of curiosity (or maybe even bewilderment) to a place where you feel confident about discussing and engaging with AI, and based on the journey we've had, I hope we're there!

We've navigated through the fundamentals, understanding how AI integrates into our daily lives—from smartphones to smart homes, work, finances, and everything in between. We've uncovered how these technologies are not just for tech wizards but everyone, including you. We've seen AI's creative side in art and music, its analytical prowess in finance and security, and its potential to revolutionize industries by making them more innovative and efficient.

Key takeaways? AI is not a distant sci-fi concept; it's here, it's now, and it's accessible. More importantly, it's a tool that you can wield to carve out opportunities and solutions, whether in your career, personal projects, or just satisfying your curiosity about the future.

Remember, understanding and leveraging AI isn't just for the select few. It's for all of us and empowers us to prepare for and shape our futures. This book aimed to demystify AI, making it as relatable as your favorite TV show and as understandable as your morning coffee routine.

Now, I want to encourage you to take the next steps. Start a simple AI project—maybe a chatbot or a basic image classifier. Join online AI communities. Engage with the platforms we discussed and use the resources mentioned throughout the chapter. Every small project and interaction adds up, deepening your understanding and skills in AI.

AI's trajectory is only going to soar. Quantum computing, ethical AI, and AI in sustainability are just the beginning. Your involvement and innovation can help steer this technology toward beneficial outcomes for our society. I hope this book lights a spark in you to be part of this exciting journey, shaping AI's future with responsibility and creativity.

From a personal standpoint, I've poured my hopes into these pages that this book serves as more than just a guide—it's the start of your lifelong adventure with AI. Sharing this knowledge with you has only strengthened my belief in the transformative power of AI education.

I'd love to hear how your journey is progressing. Share your feedback, tell me about the AI projects you've started, and let's keep the conversation going. Drop a review on Amazon, connect with us on social media, or jump into online forums linked to our book. Your insights and experiences enrich the broader dialogue about AI's role in our lives.

And finally, keep pushing forward. The road of AI is ever-evolving and full of surprises. Each step you take is a stride toward a future where technology and humanity coexist and thrive together. Here's to taking that step, learning and growing, and discovering the incredible adventures AI has in store for us all.

Keep exploring, keep innovating, and let's shape the future of AI together!

Keeping the AI Adventure Alive

Woohoo! You've made it to the end of our AI journey together. By now, you've got a solid grasp of the basics of AI and how to use it in ways that can help you and others. That's pretty awesome!

But the adventure doesn't have to end here. It's time to pass the torch and share your newfound AI wisdom with other curious minds out there.

By leaving your honest review of this book on Amazon, you'll be pointing other AI enthusiasts in the right direction, helping them find the information they're looking for. It's like passing a secret map to hidden AI treasures!

Your review is a way to keep the passion for AI alive and thriving. When we share what we've learned, we make AI more accessible for everyone. And that's exactly what you'll be doing.

Thank you for being a part of this journey and for helping spread AI love. The world of AI is kept alive by curious, generous people like you who are willing to pass on their knowledge.

>>> Click here to leave your review on Amazon and keep the AI adventure going!

Or scan the QR code:

[https://www.amazon.com/review/review-your-purchases/?asin=B0D8Z1KL4M]

Further Reading Suggestions

"Python Machine Learning"[1] by Sebastian Raschka and Vahid Mirjalili

"Hands-On Machine Learning with Scikit-Learn, Keras, and TensorFlow"[1] by Aurélien Géron

"Python Crash Course"[1] by Eric Matthes

---

1. https://amzn.to/3XrGAbx

2. https://amzn.to/3xpTTif

3. https://amzn.to/45ALWna

References

Batra, N. (2018, June 12). Comprehensive guide to build a recommendation engine in python. Analytics Vidhya. https://www.analyticsvidhya.com/blog/2018/06/comp rehensive-guide-recommendation-engine-python/

Britton, J. (2023, December 24). The top 10 AI tools of 2023, and how to use them to make more money. CNBC. https://www.cnbc.com/2023/12/24/the-top-10-ai-to ols-of-2023-and-how-to-use-them-to-make-more-money.html

Careerfoundry. (n.d.). 17 excellent AI project ideas for beginners to get started. Retrieved June 5, 2024, from https://careerfoundry.com/en/blog/data-analytics/ai -project-ideas/

Create & Learn. (n.d.). How to make your own Alexa-like chatbot with AI in Scratch. Retrieved June 5, 2024, from https://www.create-learn.us/blog/make-chatbot-wit h-ai-in-scratch/

European Space Agency. (n.d.). Artificial intelligence in space. Retrieved June 5, 2024, from https://www.esa.int/Enabling_Support/Preparing_for_the_Future/Discove ry_and_Preparation/Artificial_intelligence_in_space

Garrison Leykam. (2023, October 24). Unveiling the triumphs of AI-driven startup success stories. https://garrisonleykamphd.com/2023/10/24/unveiling-the-triump hs-of-ai-driven-startup-success-stories/

Haenlein, M., & Kaplan, A. (2019). A brief history of artificial intelligence: On the past, present, and future of artificial intelligence. California Management Review, 61(4), 5-14. https://doi.org/10.1177/0008125619864925

Hamet, P., & Tremblay, J. (2017). Artificial intelligence in medicine. Metabolism, 69, S36-S40. https://doi.org/10.1016/j.metabol.2017.01.011

Ivaturi, K. (2023, December 19). AI in healthcare: A double-edged sword? Study reveals impact on diagnostic accuracy. News-Medical.net . https://www.news-medical.net/news/20231219/AI-in-healthcare-A-double-edged -sword-Study-reveals-impact-on-diagnostic-accuracy.aspx

Jenkins, R. (n.d.). Which ethical implications of generative AI should companies focus on? Forbes. Retrieved June 5, 2024, from https://www.forbes.com/sites/forbestechcouncil/2023/10/17/which-ethical-i mplications-of-generative-ai-should-companies-focus-on/

Kukura, J. (2023, February 15). How is AI impacting and shaping the creative industries? World Economic Forum. https://www.weforum.org/agenda/2024/02 /ai-creative-industries-davos/

Lardinois, F. (2023, March 24). GPT-4 is a giant step forward, but still has significant weaknesses. TechCrunch. https://techcrunch.com/2023/03/24/gpt-4-is-a-giant-ste p-forward-but-still-has-significant-weaknesses/

Mantha, Y., & Hudson, S. (2023). How AI is supercharging money management. https://intive.com/insights/how-ai-is-supercharging-money-management

Mckinsey & Company. (2023, September 13). Is Moore's law still valid? https://www.mckinsey.com/featured-insights/themes/is-moores-law-still-valid?cid =other-eml-alt-mip-mck&hlkid=0c0cf9d5805749189.34e5b9a807b2a13&hctky=11183 712&hdpid=b04040fc-f1ef-451b-a277-30c1e21a5d20

Middleton, C. (2020, March 4). What is deep learning? A beginner's guide. Forbes. https://www.forbes.com/sites/bernardmarr/2020/03/04/what-is-deep-lea rning-a-beginners-guide/

MUO. (2023, January 11). 9 communities for beginners to learn about AI tools. https://www.makeuseof.com/online-communities-to-learn-about-ai/

Netguru. (n.d.). Using AI in finance? Consider these four ethical challenges. Re-trieved June 5, 2024, from https://www.netguru.com/blog/ai-in-finance-ethical-ch allenges

Nguyen, A., Kharosekar, A., Krishnan, S., Krishnan, S., Tate, E., Wallace, B. C., & Lease, M. (2018). Believe it or not: Designing a human-AI partnership for mixed-ini-tiative fact-checking. Proceedings of the 31st Annual ACM Symposium on User Interface Software and Technology. https://doi.org/10.1145/3242587.3242666

OrangeMantra. (2022, November 17). How AI and IoT technologies are building a smart home? https://www.orangemantra.com/blog/how-ai-and-iot-technologies-are-building-a-smart-home/

OurCrowd. (2023, January 4). Harnessing AI in climate change mitigation. https://www.ourcrowd.com/learn/harnessing-ai-in-climate-change-mitigation

Rapp, N. (2023, April 27). 4 ways AI transformed music, movies and art in 2023. Time. https://time.com/6343945/ai-music-movies-art-2023/

Readynez. (2022, April 8). Understanding AI ethics: A beginner's guide. https://www.readynez.com/en/blog/understanding-ai-ethics-a-beginner-s-guide/

Reichental, J. (2023, November 20). Quantum artificial intelligence is closer than you think. Forbes. https://www.forbes.com/sites/jonathanreichental/2023/11/20/quantum-artificial-intelligence-is-closer-than-you-think/

Reynolds, M. (2020, October 14). Ethical concerns mount as AI takes bigger decision-making role. Harvard Gazette. https://news.harvard.edu/gazette/story/2020/10/ethical-concerns-mount-as-ai-takes-bigger-decision-making-role/

Rouse, M., Botelho, B., & Tucci, L. (2023, March 20). What is GPT-4? Everything you need to know. TechTarget. https://www.techtarget.com/searchenterpriseai/definition/GPT-4

Sutton, M. (2023, May 25). 8 examples of AI personalization across industries. TechTarget. https://www.techtarget.com/searchenterpriseai/feature/8-examples-of-AI-personalization-across-industries

The Editors of Encyclopaedia Britannica. (2023, January 12). Artificial intelligence. In Encyclopædia Britannica. https://www.britannica.com/technology/artificial-intelligence

Tran, N. (2023). 9 best AI chatbot platforms: A comprehensive guide (2024). Botpress. https://botpress.com/blog/9-best-ai-chatbot-platforms

UNESCO. (n.d.). Ethics of artificial intelligence. Retrieved June 5, 2024, from https://www.unesco.org/en/artificial-intelligence/recommendation-ethics

University of Helsinki, & Reaktor. (n.d.). A free online introduction to artificial intelligence for non-experts. Elements of AI. https://www.elementsofai.com/

Upwork. (2023). The impact of AI on the job market: Key insights. https://www.upwork.com/resources/ai-job-market-impact

W., J. (2023, June 22). 11 skills you need in the AI era [Data + tips]. HubSpot Blog. https://blog.hubspot.com/marketing/skills-needed-in-ai-era

Wagner, J. (2023, April 6). Generative AI vs ChatGPT for conversational AI applications. Reveation Labs. https://www.reveation.io/blog/generative-ai-vs-chatgpt/

Weiner, R. (n.d.). 5 machine learning success stories: An inside look. CIO. https://www.cio.com/article/230692/machine-learning-success-stories.html

Yoffee, A. (2017, August 28). The history of artificial intelligence. Science in the News. https://sitn.hms.harvard.edu/flash/2017/history-artificial-intelligence/

Printed in Great Britain
by Amazon

60906864R00077